SINK OR SWIMWEAR

MY CRAZY DAYS AS AN ENTREPRENEUR
SURVIVING LIFE, PTSD, AND A CUTTHROAT INDUSTRY

Chimney Rock Publishing
26520 N. Alma School Road #835
Scottsdale, AZ 85255

ISBN: 978-1-7375729-0-9 (print)
ISBN: 978-1-7375729-1-6 (ebook)
ISBN: 978-1-7375729-2-3 (hardcover)

Sink or Swimwear is a work of nonfiction. Some names and identifying details have been changed.

Ordering Information:
Special discounts are available on quantity purchases by corporations, associations, and others. For details, contact TBD Email Address

SINK OR SWIMWEAR

MY CRAZY DAYS AS AN ENTREPRENEUR
SURVIVING LIFE, PTSD, AND A CUTTHROAT INDUSTRY

JENNIFER BERK WEISMAN

For my husband, Russell, and children, Josh and Jake.

Without you, Just Bones Boardwear would
never have been imagined.

"If you can dream it, you can do it."
—Walt Disney

TABLE OF CONTENTS

CHAPTER 1

DEER IN THE HEADLIGHTS

BEFORE THE ACCIDENT, EVERYTHING WAS falling into place. My swimwear company, Just Bones Boardwear, was taking off—the world needed functional, adjustable waist boardshorts, and I was proud to deliver. I'd just returned home from Orlando, where I'd been showing off all of our new products at Surf Expo, a major trade show. It was hard missing my sons', Josh and Jake's, first day of middle school back in New Jersey. I felt terrible about it, but I knew I couldn't pass up this chance to promote my company. The boys were understanding—they thought my new job was cool and exciting, and I did too. I was finally doing something for myself, and I *loved* it.

One local store decided to carry my boardshort line, even though I was still waiting for the patent on my adjustable waist technology to come through. A lot of people I knew had husbands or sons who would shop there. To top it off, I was close to getting an account with Hershey Park, a major theme park in central Pennsylvania, which would take my boutique business to the next level.

I had a lot riding on my company's success. My husband had supported me with my business from the outset and agreed to let me sink money into it. I didn't want to let him down.

I didn't want to let myself down, either.

Until I started Just Bones Boardwear, I was a stay-at-home mom. I got up early each day to make the kids' lunches and get them ready for school. Then we made the rounds to pick up the other kids on our carpool list. Even if my own kids were sick and stayed home, I still dragged myself out of bed to make sure the others got to school on time. I ran errands, went grocery shopping, thought about what to cook for dinner, and straightened up the house. Sometimes I went through the kids' closets and weeded out their old clothes. I often found myself running to the sports store to pick up pads, helmets, and whatever else they needed. I spent a lot of time volunteering at their school.

It seemed like I had a never-ending to-do list.

It wasn't all centered on the kids. I spent a lot of my time with other moms. Sometimes we'd hit the gym or play tennis together.

But in this cliquey, stay-at-home mom community where I found myself, things could get cutthroat. If you decided to make a change and do something different, like become a working mom, you could easily find yourself on a blacklist—no more lunch invites, no more tennis partners.

It felt like everyone's eyes were on me when I stepped out of the box to pursue my dream. Even some of my family looked on skeptically at first. I heard whispers of them wondering how I thought I could hack it in the business world with my idea and questioning why I would go back to work at all. They were waiting for me to fail, but there was no way I was going to give them that satisfaction.

Ever since I was a teen, I had always thrived on being creative, from fashioning custom-made clothes to cooking to becoming an art student in New York City. Just Bones Boardwear was born out of my desire to have adjustable boardshorts for my fast-growing sons. Despite my best efforts to find good quality boardshorts that didn't require a trip to the tailor (is that really so much to ask?), I could never find what I was looking for. So, I made my own.

Everything was coming at me so fast. Too fast. Just like the white Honda Accord.

The accident happened on September 15, 2012, in Millburn, New Jersey, when I went to town that afternoon to run a couple errands. I had just parted ways with my husband and sons at a menswear store in Livingston, the next town over. They decided to go for lunch while I went to pick up a framed feature article on Just Bones Boardwear at a photo shop in Millburn.

The boys' b'nai mitzvah—like a bar mitzvah but for the both of them—was only one month away, and they went to try on their suits to make sure the latest alterations were good. They were so excited for their big day. We planned to meet up again after the boys had finished lunch.

We had moved to Short Hills, in Millburn township, when I became pregnant with our twin sons. It had safe streets with colonial brick houses, big backyards with green lawns for the kids to play, and a terrific school system. It was also a quick train ride or drive into New York City. That made it easy to get to work and doctors' appointments and gave us access to entertainment in the Big Apple. Millburn, a neighboring town, had dining, shopping, theatre, and a train station.

I parked in the municipal lot by the bicycle shop as usual, checking to make sure I had some change for the meter. My cell phone rang. It was my mom, but I decided I would call her back later and let her go to voice mail.

It was unseasonably warm for September in New Jersey and a beautiful, sunny day. I was wearing just a gray tank, army-green shorts, and a pair of Havaianas flip-flops. I put on my sunglasses, tucked my cell in my back pocket, and dropped quarters in the meter. I remember hoping that the day of the boys' b'nai mitzvah would be this nice. I wished I had gone for lunch with my hubby and the boys and taken advantage of such a gorgeous day—soon we would have snow. But I had so much to do in the follow-up of the trade show. I decided I'd swing by the Starbucks on the corner after the photo shop. My stomach was rumbling.

I stood at the corner waiting for the walk sign to flash green before stepping out into the crosswalk so I could cross Main Street. I got three-quarters of the way across and then *BOOM!* Like a huge explosion.

Suddenly, it was lights out.

When I came to, I didn't understand what had happened.

A guy was kneeling in front of me saying he was a doctor. He told me a woman had hung a really quick left turn at the light and hit me with her car. The impact threw me out of the crosswalk, and I landed on my head and shoulder.

"I'm going to help you," the doctor said. "I heard the crash."

Still, I didn't understand what was happening. I had gone into shock. The doctor was holding my head, and I didn't realize until later at the hospital that I had a huge head wound. When I looked down, I saw that blood covered my arms, my top, and my shorts. My flip-flops and sunglasses had flown off. My cell phone was somewhere. The contents of my purse—my wallet, house keys, and loose change—were everywhere.

Then, suddenly, my husband was beside me, and the boys were staring at me from the sidewalk like deer in headlights. All I could think then was, *Why are they here?*

The ambulance took me to the Morristown Hospital emergency room where they handle the trauma cases. The ride seemed to take forever, and throughout it, I was extremely aware of the trauma board and cervical collar supporting me on the gurney. The paramedics spoke to me continuously, telling me I would be alright, as though they were trying to keep me alert.

I just wanted out of there.

CHAPTER 2

EUREKA

M Y LIFE CHANGED DURING A family vacation about 18 months before the accident. It started off like one of those *National Lampoon's Vacation* movies, where everything that could go wrong did go wrong.

A huge winter storm slammed New York before we left. There was so much snow on our roof that water eventually leaked through it and into the kitchen through the recessed lighting. It took hours to shovel enough snow off to avoid the risk of the roof caving in. Because of the storm, our flight was pushed back three days. We kept trying to call the resort to reschedule and coordinate with the airline.

This was not the relaxing, fun start to Winter Break we'd imagined. But we were determined. My husband Russell and I had been planning to take Josh and Jake to the Atlantis in the Bahamas since forever.

Luckily, we were able to take care of our roof before we left. Five guys climbed up there, shoveling pounds of snow off for the better part of a day. I just prayed it would not snow again while we were away or before they could check the roof out for any major damage. I had already made plans for our kitchen ceiling repairs. The boys busied themselves with friends of theirs who were also stuck at home from the storm. Everyone's Winter Break vacations were postponed like ours.

We were finally able to rebook and get on to a flight to Nassau. Newark Airport was a complete mess, with luggage carts cluttering the check-in area and long lines of travelers everywhere. We were worried we wouldn't make the flight when it came down to it, but fortunately we did.

When we landed, we shuffled out to pick up our luggage. But it wasn't there. No one on our flight got their luggage that day. The line for customer service seemed to snake around the entire baggage claim. This was supposed to be paradise, and so far, it was anything but.

However, determined to make the best of it, we stopped by a drug store to pick up all those little things you need when you travel, such as toothpaste, toothbrushes, suntan lotion, and shampoo. Fortunately, our driver from the airport knew where to take us and was especially helpful.

Later, after checking in, we stopped by the resort village to pick up swimsuits. After all, the whole point of going on the vacation was to be able to swim in and enjoy the warm, tropical water and get away from the teeth-chattering New York winter. It was easy to find swimwear for me and Russell. But we couldn't find anything that fit the boys!

If it fit around the waist, it was too small everywhere else. If it fit them other places, it was too big around their waists.

I was so frustrated they didn't have adjustable sizes so the swim shorts would just stay on better. How was something like that not for sale? I mean, how many thousands of people searched the stores for that very thing and came up empty handed?

I kept thinking how silly it was. The kids had adjustable clothing when they were younger. When they were toddlers, they had adjustable pants and shorts. Why was that so challenging for swimwear? Why were volley shorts the only things available at the shops?

This is something that needs to be fixed. I bet I could do it better.

After all, I designed my own prom dress and created custom graphic tees. At that point, I didn't know how to do it, but I knew I could.

That was the spark that lit the fire that became Just Bones Boardwear—named after my love of all things skull and crossbones.

The day I spent wandering around looking for what I needed marked the beginning of my journey to figure out how to walk the tightrope of running a business, running a household, and fighting giants when everything around me rained shit.

When I got home from that vacation, I went to the drawing board. Literally. I drew up different designs I'd imagined since that day of looking for boardshorts, crumpling up what wouldn't work until I found something that would. I had never come across anything remotely similar to what I envisioned making.

It felt good to tap into my creative side again. It felt like an eternity since I'd attended the Fashion Institute of Technology (FIT), majoring in textiles, with hopes of some type of career in the fashion world.

At that point, I hadn't given any thought to the future. I didn't go into it with the goal to build a fashion empire or thinking I'd change lives. I really just wanted to solve this problem. I had an idea, and I wanted to see it come to fruition.

By the time I got the design just right, it was a hot, humid summer in New York. One sweltering day, I took to the Garment District in the heart of Midtown Manhattan to find the perfect fabric.

There is a wide array of businesses nestled in the Garment District including textile, trimming, accessory, apparel, and even furriers. I knew if I needed anything from buttons to zippers to boardshort fabric, I could find it somewhere in the rows of stores up and down the numerous streets.

Many stores in the district only sell wholesale, which meant I'd need a tax ID—something I didn't yet have—proving I was shopping for a business, not just for myself. So, the first order of business was making sure they would sell to me as an individual, for my personal use.

Next was to find a store that sold swimwear fabric, which was easier said than done. Many told me they didn't sell it. Others tried to pass off the kind of fabric you'd use for athletic wear or gymnastic outfits as swim fabric—often it would be hot pink, sparkly, stretchy, and certainly *not* made for wear in the water or exposure to chlorine or the sun.

Many bolts of fabric were sold as remnants and thus were not refundable or returnable. You had to know what you wanted.

For example, when you place an order with a factory to produce the exact fabric you want, there is an MOQ, minimum order quantity—a minimum amount of fabric yardage is produced. This is typical with most factories. Soon, you have thousands of yards of unfinished fabric called greige, which is then processed for RFD (ready for dyeing). Lastly, the greige goes through digital printing, or screen printing, and becomes your custom-made fabric. Perhaps you had to pay the factory to produce 5,000 yards of fabric, their MOQ, but after all the cutting, sewing, finishing, and packaging is done for your orders, you only used 3,500 yards of fabric. You still have a lot of fabric leftover, but you can't really use it to create more product. Many companies will then sell the remnant fabric to the Garment District to recoup their money. However, some companies, like ours, only produce, cut, and sew to order so they do not have leftover fabric. In addition, they do not want anyone else to use their exclusive fabric designs for other apparel goods.

The fabric shops didn't exactly have labels explicitly describing the fabric's fiber composition. They were not like Mood Fabrics, where I had not yet had the exquisite pleasure of shopping. But even without content labels, I found I could draw from my experience of studying textiles. The best way of knowing when I'd found the type of fabric I needed was by feeling it. I tugged at a piece to determine if it was 4-way or 2-way stretch and kept a sharp eye out for swimwear fabric.

Each time I wanted to inspect a new fabric, someone from the shop had to help me get to it. The bolts of fabric weigh a ton, and some were stacked on high shelves, so I couldn't do it by myself.

I must have gone to 15 or 20 stores looking for the right fabric. Every time I made it back inside to an air-conditioned space, I felt a wave of relief. It was the dead of summer with temperatures and humidity hitting the mid-90s. My maxi dress was beginning to stick to me as I walked.

After trekking through the district for hours, sweating to death in the 95-degree heat, I saw it: a green, camouflage print fabric. I reached out to touch it, brushing my fingers along the soft, stretchy polyester. I knew right away it was definitely usable for swimwear.

Because it had been so hard to find, I bought a lot of it. At that point, I didn't know how much I'd need to make one perfect prototype.

I walked away with 10 yards of this remnant fabric I had been fortunate to finally hunt down. I also bought buttonhole elastic, Velcro, and a variety of buttons at a trim shop. Carrying it back to the car, all bundled into a large plastic bag, was a workout in and of itself in the oppressive heat, but I no longer noticed it. I was too excited to get to work and make this new swimwear idea come to life.

Later, I met up with a college girlfriend of mine, Vivian, to talk about the project over dinner. I showed her the fabric and told her my idea—but first she had to swear to secrecy. She was one of my best friends since college, so I trusted her, but it was still uncomfortable. I was basically putting her in a position where she couldn't tell another soul what I was planning on doing.

As we sat down to eat at a nice restaurant downtown, I pushed my food around on my plate.

"Do you think it could work?" I asked.

Vivian had worked in the garment industry since graduating FIT, so she knew a thing or two about launching new products and what it took to do so.

"I think it's a great idea," she said.

I breathed a sigh of relief. Russell believed in me too. He thought it was a great idea. But he's my husband! He's *supposed* to think I have good ideas!

She was the second person to believe in me. Maybe I could really do this.

In the following weeks, I awkwardly handed out nondisclosure agreements to everyone—including my friends—who'd either heard about my project from me or who was a part of it. This felt funny, and I worried some of the people I trusted most would be offended I was asking them to sign this piece of paper. But my lawyer insisted, and I listened. Being a lawyer's daughter, I knew it was important to protect my idea, even if it felt strange. Thankfully, no one seemed upset.

Struggling under the weight of the enormous load of camouflage fabric, yards of Velcro, and elastic, I walked in to see the seamstress with my sketches in hand.

It took a couple tries, but the seamstress eventually nailed it. When I held the boardshorts in my hands for the first time, I felt a rush of validation.

I can do this. This will make moms' lives easier. This product will sell.

While the patent was pending, word started to get out about my product in the mom groups at school. One woman invited me to come sell my boardshorts at a school fundraiser boutique.

Even though I could feel the silent judgment radiating out of their eyeballs (*Doesn't this little project take time away from your children? How can you possibly pay enough attention to them if you have this other thing in your life? What if you fail?*), it would be the first opportunity I had to test out and sell my product to anyone. So, I accepted the invitation.

Some of the other moms saw my boardshort samples and decided to order a pair. For them, it was no big deal. They could drop $49 on a pair of boardshorts and not think twice. They, after all, were sure to support every charity posted up in school—and that's what I was then. *I* was charity at this point.

That's what I was trying to get away from.

They all pretended to be happy for me, but many of them resented me for breaking away from the pack.

One woman said something to me I'll never forget. It sounded like a compliment, but it was steeped in venom. She worked part-time, mostly because she enjoyed what she did and to have spending money of her own. Her husband made a bunch of money, and she spent most of her free time hanging out with other moms and getting manis and pedis when she wasn't taking care of the kids.

"Oh, look at you, aren't you always reinventing yourself?" she said.

My husband told me to take it as a compliment, but that was as backhanded as they come.

Back then, I felt like I had a lot to prove. I wanted my business to be successful. I wanted my husband and my sons to be proud of me. Most of all, I wanted to do something for myself, and do it *well*.

CHAPTER 3

SPICE THINGS UP

I TAPPED INTO MY CREATIVE SIDE nearly every weeknight by making delicious meals for my family. I loved to try new things and go all out to prepare something tasty. I took pleasure in cooking elaborate, gourmet meals for guests too.

One New Year's Eve, I planned a festive, full-course dinner and invited two other couples over. I adore making various soufflés, but on this occasion, I decided to switch things up. The menu was complete with a charcuterie and cheese board to start, followed by seared duck breast in a spiced cranberry-orange sauce, Hasselback sweet potatoes topped with pecans, thyme, and Parmesan, and fresh popovers. For dessert, I served homemade crème brûlée. Upon arrival, I greeted our guests with a Bellini cocktail, made with fresh blackberry-thyme simple syrup and Prosecco. Because it was a holiday dinner, I decorated the table with a gold runner over a black tablecloth, gold chargers, and a crisp white floral arrangement. There were 3D gold stars hanging above the table, and I'd set about some humorous New Year's Eve hats and masks.

I did it all for enjoyment, so I was honestly shocked when my friend told me that dinner had been as good as any Michelin-star restaurant she had dined in. That made it so gratifying, as well as the wonderful evening we all had ringing in the New Year.

Russell once told me he thought some people were nervous to have us over to their place for dinner after I had cooked for them. I never meant for that to be the case! I just found gratification in cooking, and I wanted others to be able to enjoy it too. I found delight in trying out the greatest and latest cooking paraphernalia, such as a French mandoline, immersion blender, microplane, and chef torch, and techniques like sous vide. For me, it made cooking even more interesting and exciting.

Recently, Russell and I had a friend and his wife over for dinner—he happened to be a bar manager of a high-end resort restaurant, and she happened to be a chef at a country club.

Suddenly, I understood why people felt intimidated! I wanted them to enjoy the meal at our home, so I went all out. I made part of the dessert in advance over the weekend, I made my own simple syrup for the cocktails, and I got ready to cook the fresh duck breasts sous vide. I had always simply pan seared my duck breasts in the past. Nervous now that the potatoes would be overdone—our guests had gotten turned around inside our large neighborhood for a half hour, which threw off my cooking time. Never a good thing for a perfect dinner. When they arrived, I quickly mixed cocktails, complemented with fresh fruit garnish. Waiting for a sign of approval was sheer suspense since he was a master mixologist.

There was more pressure than usual that meal, especially because she was a skilled chef. But they both seemed to thoroughly enjoy everything I had prepared. We laughed, ate, and drank until the late-night hours. Later, after they left, Russell told me that while I was preparing dessert, both had commented the duck was restaurant quality and as good as they had eaten anywhere! To top it off, our friend is 6'5" and has a hard time finding boardshorts that are both long enough for his tall frame and fit well. When I told him about Just Bones Boardwear, he was very interested. He was especially thrilled when I gave him a pair to try out and told me how perfectly they fit. *This is why I love what I do!*

Sometimes, I'd even teach others how to cook.

One of my girlfriends came from a big Italian family, but she didn't know how to cook. It just wasn't something her family passed down. She asked me to teach her how to make a couple traditional Italian dishes, so I did! There we were in our 20s: me, the girl from Miami raised on seafood and sunshine, teaching the girl from Long Island how to make homemade lasagna and chicken Parmesan—real comfort food. We didn't make that in Florida.

When I cook, I'm all about the presentation. I love paying attention to the details of how a dish is plated, how it tastes, and what wine pairs best with it. I love to create an entire dining experience. You could call it my passion.

Before I started the business, I never minded going to the grocery store, cleaning, cooking, or anything like that. I didn't mind driving my kids around to their various activities. I loved my boys, and I loved spending time with them. Truly, it was the other adults who, at times, made life as a stay-at-home mom unappealing.

When my boys were in elementary school, they played sports like basketball, baseball, and lacrosse. You know, little league and other team sports. It was supposed to be fun, but so many parents took it way too seriously.

Parents would scream at these poor referees or umpires—some who were only in high school, by the way—like lunatics. These parents got it into their heads that their children were going on to be professional athletes and their future careers were riding on one call. The whole thing was so ridiculous. It felt like so many parents were living vicariously through their kids. Worse than that, though, was the insufferable gossip. The stay-at-home mom community was always talking about something or someone around me. At times, I felt like I was living in a reality TV show.

To this day, I still don't know what is so gratifying about witnessing or taking part in another person's misery. I never heard them sitting around saying good things about anybody. They didn't want to lift anyone up.

I was glad to leave that petty bullshit behind. When I did launch my business, I was too busy to know what was going on with anyone. I didn't know what the latest gossip was. They could have been talking about me, and I wouldn't know. It was perfect.

CHAPTER 4

MICKEY MOUSE DEGREE

MY PARENTS GOT DIVORCED WHEN I was three years old and we lived in Miami. My mother, who'd been so young when they got married, moved back to the Atlanta suburbs where she grew up. She decided to go back to school to be a radiology technician. I lived with my dad, spending a lot of time with our live-in housekeeper while my dad was at work. I vaguely remember first meeting my stepmom. She gave me a Disney toy when my dad was first dating her. It was a black top hat that Mickey Mouse popped out of—it may be one of the nicest memories I have of her.

After my dad remarried, I briefly lived with him, my stepmom, and my four older half-sisters. My half-sisters were jealous that I got to spend so much time with our dad. They thought that for some reason, because I'd grown up with him and they moved in later on, things were better for me. We never got along that well. My dad used to get frustrated when we'd all sit down for dinner because someone would always be fighting. All he wanted was for us to get together and get along. He wanted us to be this big, happy family, but we weren't. Ultimately, my half sisters moved to New York with their mother, where she was born and raised. We didn't grow up together in the same household for most of our lives, and there was constant friction between us—sadly even as adults.

My dad was strict about school and grades—at least with the girls in the family. After five girls, he was so overjoyed when he finally had a son, he tended to be more lenient with the boys. He expected us all to get straight As. However, he wasn't the kind to offer a reward for the accomplishment like some families do by giving their kids a couple bucks or taking them out to a special dinner if they got good grades—he just expected us to get them. So, I worked hard to get straight As to win his approval.

Growing up, I studied ballet. I danced in countless recitals and productions, but he was never in the crowd. He never saw me on stage. I think it's partly because that's just how men in his generation were raised. When I'd invite him to a performance, he'd say, "When you're a prima ballerina, I'll come watch you."

Other kids' parents came to watch them. In prep school, I remember my friends' parents going to every swim competition, lacrosse game, football game, and theater performance.

By the time I was older, I didn't really think about it. I was just accustomed to the fact my dad didn't come. He didn't come when I was younger; why would he come now? If it was only a high school performance, it wouldn't measure up to his standards.

Regardless, I kept working hard in other creative fields, honing my craft as I took art classes along with ballet. I also discovered that I liked cooking. I took a few cooking classes when I was in middle school and often helped my stepmom in the kitchen. The one thing I can give her credit for was making me confident in the kitchen and feeding my passion for cooking. She was a gourmet cook and entertained a lot.

When I came home on the weekends from Pine Crest Preparatory School, I channeled some of my creativity into making custom graphic tees. It was the 80s, and I loved the torn, off-the-shoulder *Flashdance* style then. I bought some white Hanes T-shirts, cut them to fall off the shoulder, and used puffy fabric paint for my freehand designs. Puffy paint came in this squishy bottle that reminds me of a pastry bag you'd squeeze frosting out of. I painted 3D designs like huge lips, hearts, and rainbows on the shirts—it was all very 80s.

My stepmom thought it was so cool I'd made one for myself that she asked me to make one for her too. So, I did. She wore it to the gym for one of her workout classes—the kind you might find Jane Fonda leading. When she came home, she told me her friends wanted shirts too and that they'd pay me to make them.

As a teenager, I thought that was the best compliment to receive about my designs. I don't remember thinking much about what that could mean for the rest of my life. I just thought it was nice to make some spending money doing something I enjoyed.

When I wasn't working on the tees, I spent a couple weekends painting my bedroom wall to look like the beach, complete with the ocean on the horizon, the sunset, and palm trees. It made my room feel like an escape when I needed it.

I took sewing and patternmaking classes during high school as a hobby, though I never actually enjoyed sewing at a sewing machine. For some reason, it seemed so mundane to me. I could sit and complete short projects, like hand-sewing Barbie doll outfits all day when I was younger. I could hem my clothing and sew on trims, but I didn't love the sewing machine. I did make an entire outfit using a sewing machine as part of my patternmaking class, and I was proud of it, yet it was not at the top of my list of creative activities I was fond of.

My mom, on the other hand, would sit at the sewing machine for hours and make all kinds of things. My grandmother would too—she'd reupholster her chairs, her couches, and her drapes whenever she got the urge. I can recall my grandmother sitting at her Singer sewing machine for hours in their finished basement when I visited as a young teen. She had an entire section set up with her special needles, threads, and fabrics. The buzzing of the machine was calming. It had its own mechanical rhythm, and I liked to sit and have conversations with my grandmother while she sewed.

Every summer, until they moved to New Orleans, my two first cousins and I would go stay with our grandparents in Marietta, Georgia, for two weeks. We loved exploring Kennesaw Mountain National Battlefield Park with our grandfather or running around the neighborhood with other kids our age. Somehow, I would manage to convince my cousins to learn entire lyrics to songs, dress up, and put on "shows" with me for our grandparents in the evenings. We performed songs from movies like *Grease* and *Saturday Night Fever*. I cherished those summers we spent together. I was close with my cousins—often, they felt more like brothers to me.

In my senior year, I designed my own prom dress. Even though I didn't sew it myself, I considered the design to be the epitome of glam. It was shiny black satin with a pleated sash waistband. The hourglass silhouette was trimmed in black and gold lace, and the bodice was a bustier. The dress came down to a little above my knees. It was different from the dresses everyone else wore that year, and that's exactly what I wanted. Of course, that's why I also had to show up to the prom with a college boy.

Despite all the effort I put into designing that dress, we didn't stay at prom for very long. I wasn't really a prom type of girl. I wouldn't necessarily say I was a rebel, but I never wanted to do what everyone else was doing. I always wanted to try something new and interesting.

That carried over into many other aspects of my life. I would do things on a whim because I simply wanted to do them. One weekend in high school, I decided to make bagels because I'd never made them before. I had no clue that you had to boil the bagels before you baked them. But I decided to do something, so I did it. The bagels actually turned out great, and I was pleased with myself that I'd tackled that recipe from scratch.

Even now, I still do amusing things like that.

When Russell and I first moved to Arizona in December of 2018, I discovered we had an abundance of prickly pear cacti around our house. When they bore fruit that first summer, there were so many prickly pears, all so bright and juicy. I decided to try and make some prickly pear margaritas. I read several different recipes and combined the methods I thought would work the best. But wow, was it time consuming and hazardous.

Once I picked the prickly pears—which was an endeavor in and of itself—I had to hold each one over the burner of the gas stove with barbecue tongs. That made the spines pop off. Then I had to simmer the fruit in water for 50 minutes before cutting them open and scraping all the flesh out. My hands were so red. The juice was everywhere! I could have tie-dyed a shirt from all that pink juice. Then I put the flesh of the pears through a strainer and juiced them.

The cocktails were amazing, but it took two hours to make four margaritas for our happy hour. That was way too much work, but once I get started, I don't give up. If I start a project, I have to see it through to the end.

As I look back on my teenage years, I wish I'd had the patience to sit down at the sewing machine and be dedicated enough to use it for more complicated projects, like my grandmother did. There is so much you can do with a sewing machine. I often think about my grandmother, who could do so much, *make* so much. It must be nice to have that alone time with the only sound being the rhythmic humming of the sewing machine. I think about my dad's French girlfriend at one time, who would make little drapes for the windows of his boat with matching pillows. She could make just about anything at a sewing machine too.

If I could go back in time, I would tell myself to take every class seriously in my major at FIT, even if it seemed dreary. I know now that there was so much to learn and so much I'd use later in life. At the time, though, I found our looming class tedious—we learned how to construct woven fabric ourselves on a hand loom in class—and could not imagine what on earth I would do with that skill later after I graduated. However, practical knowledge about different fabrics and how they are created is useful. Woven fabric is a textile typically created on a mechanical loom consisting of many threads woven together, while knit fabric is created on a knitting machine that uses interlacing loops to create fabric different in composition. This knowledge proved to be extremely beneficial to me years later when I had to deal with factories and fabric samples for my swimwear business.

When I was in school, I had to do all sorts of projects that seemed irrelevant to me at the time. I remember one project involved picking a magazine photo to replicate. To do this, we had to use a sheet of graph paper, then flip through the magazine to find colors from other photos that matched. The idea was to fill in the graph paper with small cutout squares from different magazine photos, pasted onto each square, to mirror the original image.

It was *so* time consuming. It seemed like such a pain in the butt then. As I spent hours cutting out tiny pieces of paper, I found myself wondering what the point of it all was. But I stuck with it and completed the task. But if I were to speculate now, it had a lot to do with learning about color, matching Pantones, and blending—something I would later deal with extensively.

That same work ethic served me well as I laid the groundwork for a career in the fashion industry. An art teacher at Pine Crest encouraged me to apply to the Fashion Institute of Technology. At the time, I didn't realize my stepmother had *also* attended FIT for college. So, of course, she was enthusiastic for me to apply—it would give her the perfect excuse to visit New York City and do some shopping. She wasn't really excited about me and my future.

That was one of the few times in my life I truly doubted myself. I was living at boarding school, and my dad and stepmom weren't exactly a cheerleading squad. They didn't wait with bated breath every time I opened a college admissions letter.

I felt nervous about trying to get into FIT. It was a big undertaking for me to figure out the whole application process. My art teacher looked at a few pieces in my portfolio and told me he thought I could do it. If my work was good enough for an art teacher, if he thought I could get in, then maybe I *did* have a shot.

To apply, I had to submit a portfolio showing a range of my artistic work, including mixed media art. I showcased the bedroom wall mural I'd painted, the graphic tees I made, and even a video game cake I hand decorated, as well as the custom-painted cake board for it, to prove I could do several different types of creative work.

To my surprise and relief, I was accepted! I wish I could thank my high school art teacher today, but I don't know how to contact him or where he grew up. All I remember is his crooked nose born from playing many years of ice hockey.

Pine Crest made a big deal about all the seniors and where they planned to go to college. When my art teacher learned I was accepted into FIT, he made sure to congratulate me.

I expected my dad to finally be proud of me too. But he wasn't. And he didn't want me to go to college in Florida or in New York City. He called it the "Mickey Mouse" college. He didn't think I'd benefit from attending school there. He didn't think I could get a decent paying job after graduation if I went.

Despite his reservations, I did attend FIT for a while. I majored in textile design and loved it, but eventually I changed my major and even changed schools. One weekend during my second semester at FIT, my stepmom came to visit me and go shopping in New York. Even though we didn't get along well, I swallowed my pride and let her stay with me. She even took me to one of her favorite restaurants, The Russian Tea Room. That weekend, my dorm room phone startled us awake in the middle of the night.

My dad had been admitted to the hospital after suffering a major heart attack. The voice on the line said it was vital my stepmom return to North Carolina right away. At the time, my dad was spending most of his time there during the real estate boom because he was general counsel for a huge real estate developer. I didn't know it then, but he and my stepmom had already separated and were headed for divorce. Being seemingly expendable to my half-sisters since I was *only* in college, they pressured me to leave New York City and live with our dad. He required triple bypass heart surgery and would otherwise be living alone afterward. I was elected by the four of them to take care of him during his lengthy recovery. No one asked me about my feelings or about my plans for the future. After all, I was merely a freshman. Kind of ironic considering how jealous they were that I spent so much time with our dad when we were kids. So, I transferred colleges, changed my major, and moved to North Carolina, which could not be more different than New York City. Part of me was devastated to leave New York, a city I dearly loved. Equally, part of me didn't love being creative on demand every single day in class at FIT, but it didn't kill me.

My dad was hopeful I would do something bigger with my life now that I had changed schools. He clearly thought I would get a better education and job attending college in North Carolina.

"I'm so happy you're not going to that Mickey Mouse college anymore," he'd say. He never considered I didn't have much say in the matter, just that the upshot was I left New York City.

Maybe that's why he could never bring himself to congratulate me on the two patents I was awarded for my adjustable waist boardshort design. It's exactly what he didn't want me to do with my life. Never mind that living in North Carolina with my dad was not exactly the plan that *I had* for my life.

CHAPTER 5

YOU CAN'T HAVE YOUR CAKE

AFTER COLLEGE, I JUMPED AT the chance to return to New York. I got my first job at Knoll Furniture, a design firm that produces everything from tables and desks to seating, from office systems to textiles. I worked my way up from an entry-level position to one in their marketing department. The company focuses on creating modern designs built to complement our modern lives, though it also maintains a healthy respect for the classics—many pieces are on display in museum collections today.

If I had never worked there, I wouldn't have met the coworker at Knoll who was basically responsible for Russell and I meeting and subsequently marrying. One holiday weekend, she invited me to her parents' place in Chappaqua, New York, a suburb of the city. It was relaxing to see something other than concrete and skyscrapers. Her brother happened to be visiting from Chicago that same weekend. He met Russell years before during a Club

Med vacation. A few years later, he played matchmaker and introduced Russell and me on a blind date.

Despite the good that came from working at Knoll Furniture, there was plenty of bad.

It was the '90s, so a long time before the Me Too movement would take off. I was sexually harassed twice at the company—even though I went to HR, they didn't do much about it.

Beyond the blatant harassment, there was a weird culture at the company. So many of the employees were having affairs with each other, and no one thought much of it. Many companies frown on employees fraternizing with each other.

I wasn't sad to leave that experience behind. Eventually, I found my way to a company that organized and marketed conferences for high-level executives. There, I specialized in brainstorming and coordinating finance conferences.

Every now and then, I would show my dad some of the brochures I had written and designed for my conferences, and I swear if he did not nitpick every single one. There was always something he thought I could have done better. It used to really annoy me—I wasn't particularly asking for his opinion, but he gave it anyway.

The conferences were big and successful, and were held at resorts all across the U.S. I enjoyed what I did. I'd started with the company when it was small, and my experience grew alongside it. There was flexibility to change and adjust my role and tackle new challenges as they emerged. I traveled a lot and juggled many different responsibilities, including selling sponsorships to prominent companies in the finance sector.

But when I found out I was pregnant with twins, I told my boss I was resigning and that I wasn't coming back.

My dad had married stay-at-home moms, so I don't think he considered my decision to leave my job unusual. But that didn't stop him from making bad jokes anyway.

During my pregnancy, I gained about 40 pounds. Right after the kids were born, when my dad saw me he said, "You're still fat!" I was very upset by that. I'm not an elastic band that can snap back in three days! Truthfully, I don't know how I didn't grow up to be anorexic or bulimic. The ballet weigh-ins did nothing for my self-confidence either. If you gained a pound or two, they would berate you. Now that I'm older, I can firmly say that I don't think that's healthy, especially for girls at such an impressionable age.

Looking back, I think my dad's attitude to body image was influenced by both my mom and my stepmother. He married women who'd both modeled a little bit. They were both very slim and vigilant about staying in shape. Thus, he was accustomed to being around women who took care of themselves and paid a lot of attention to how they looked.

My mom ate very healthfully. She was never overweight. And she didn't want me to be either. She always wore the same size as me and could easily fit into my clothes—not necessarily a good thing when I was older and she wanted to "shop" in my closet during visits.

She often made comments to me about eating snacks after school. I loved peanut butter and banana sandwiches when I was younger, so I'd make them for myself. If she saw me, she'd always say something about it.

"Jen, you shouldn't be eating that; you'll gain weight," she'd say.

My stepmom was exactly the same way. Growing up, we didn't have potato chips, candy, or any junk food in the house. Whenever I stayed over at a friend's house or went to sleepaway camp, I had a field day. I almost could not control myself. It was like I hit the jackpot, the mother lode (*Willy Wonka and the Chocolate Factory* comes to mind).

My stepmom was also strict about food in other ways. What she cooked, she expected you to eat—no exceptions. She was a gourmet cook, and she would occasionally prepare some out-of-the-box things like escargot and turtle steak. We were her guinea pigs if she wanted to try out a new recipe. As a kid, I can only remember looking at that turtle steak with disgust. I just couldn't do it.

I had a couple tricks up my sleeve to choke down what I could. I would often slather some undesirable thing with ketchup and take a big gulp of milk after to make progress. But she knew all about tricks, like spitting gross food into a napkin and discretely tossing it in the trash when no one was looking or trying to feed it to the dog. Those I couldn't get away with.

She made me sit at the kitchen table alone for hours looking at my food if I couldn't eat it.

"If you don't eat it for dinner, it will be there for breakfast," she'd say. Many nights, I'd fall asleep on the table because I'd sit there so long.

My mom could rival her for strictness at the table. At one point, she was married to a doctor who grew up on a military base, so they were both uncompromising about food. She'd often make liver and onions for dinner and force me to eat it. They believed wholeheartedly this was a healthy dinner, full of protein. There was definitely no junk food in *that* house.

Who does that to their kids?

I may have a more exotic pallet than some of my friends, but even now, I don't eat or cook anything I think is atypical, like turtle or rabbit. The thought of eating Thumper still bothers me.

I decided I would never do that to my kids. I always want the cooking *and* the eating experience to be pleasant for all involved. If they didn't like something, I never forced my kids to eat it.

During my first year at boarding school, I gained the "freshman 15" because I was finally allowed to eat whatever I wanted, whenever I wanted. And you know what? It wasn't a big deal. I lost the weight the following year—but my dad never missed the chance to call me chubby.

When I launched my bikini line, I went out of my way to have models on the runway who weren't stick thin. I didn't want to promote that image. I wanted to advertise a healthy figure with curves.

Occasionally, I got stuck with last-minute replacement models who were super skinny, and it pissed me off. It wasn't the look I wanted for my brand. I never wanted to put girls on the runway who were emaciated and promoted a negative body image. It's not healthy.

But my dad had an opinion about everything. Even as I surpassed the expectations I had for myself in business, he never said he was proud of me.

Even though my father's lack of support stung, I was determined not to let that get in the way of accomplishing the goals I set for myself. I continued to work hard and grow brand awareness.

———————

Russell and I talked over my career plans. As the boys were starting back at school, he acknowledged it might be good for me to go back to work. But, instead of going back to the company I had left, where I had made a six-figure salary, Russell agreed to support me as I started my own company.

I think at the time he thought it would be a nice hobby. That it would give me something to do in my free time. Little did he know then how much this business would change both of our lives.

We used some money from the sale of Russell's family business to get started. The company was very niche. The factory made insulated refrigerated doors, the kind you'd see underneath countertops for wine or beverage storage. They also made doors for supermarkets and for large soda machines, some extremely specialized. At one point, they even worked with the kitchen appliance company Sub-Zero on their wine storage design and made sliders for Starbucks' pastry sections. If you've ever seen those big vending machines with arms and a frosted glass design, or cases that have double-insulated glass for refrigeration, that was Russell's company.

His uncle and grandfather started the family business. Back then, they had manufactured gaskets. Then they started to make glass doors. That's when Russell's dad got involved.

Then some years later, over summer breaks during high school and college, Russell himself worked in the factory. After graduating college, Russell went to law school and practiced law for around five years.

Over that time, his dad kept asking him if he wanted to do more with his life, even after he was practicing law. "Don't you want to come into business with me?" he asked. "If you don't like it, you can always go back to law."

Russell was reluctant at first, but he eventually gave in. That turned out to be a great move for him—he liked working with his dad far more than he liked law. In fact, Russell turned out to be a skillful businessman and was instrumental in growing the company considerably from what it had been on his arrival.

Russell worked with his dad for many years, until the kids were in elementary school. Around then, one of their biggest competitors, a huge company in California, offered to buy their business. Russell agreed to stay on as a consultant for three years. He even went to Shanghai for them once. Part of the deal for the sale and Russell staying on was that the Californian company agreed to keep using their New Jersey factory and staff. When he sold the business, Russell made them promise not to shut down the factory.

But after those three years were up, that's exactly what they did. Everyone who had worked for Russell and his dad lost their jobs. I'd never seen him so angry. He almost couldn't live with what had happened. All those people he cared so much about were out of a job, and he felt like it was his fault. Russell shouldered guilt for a long time.

With the sale, though, we never *had* to go back to work. Russell was in his mid-40s, and I was even younger, in my mid-30s. I could have done nothing but shop, play tennis, and work out. I could have been a stay-at-home mom for the rest of my life, and Russell could have filled his days playing golf at the country club. We could have traveled the world! It could have been like a second honeymoon!

But this was my chance to see if I could truly solve a problem *and* run a business if I put my mind to it.

In the early days of Just Bones Boardwear, I always had a lingering feeling of guilt, like I needed to earn back the money that Russell had put into my company. After all, it was his hard-earned money, which he got from selling the business that he built with his dad. It was part of his legacy too.

Besides that, everyone knows that when you first start a business it can take several years to make something of it—unless you have an amazing product that catches on fire or insane overnight success like Facebook.

We'd been on a good trajectory shortly after I started Just Bones Boardwear, but soon we were sinking money into huge legal fees with a trademark lawsuit. Then the accident knocked us completely off course.

Once I couldn't work full-time or put my full attention into the business, it was hard to catch up to where we should have been and get back on track. Eventually, we did come out on top, but even now, I can't help but wonder where we'd be today had the accident never happened. The only reason I kept going was sheer willpower—and the patents. I believed in what we were doing. I knew if I believed in it, I could sell it. I was a good salesperson. I wouldn't have been making six figures selling finance companies on conferences if I wasn't.

But more than that, I still had something to prove. I had already done trade shows. I had already heard from so many people that this was an awesome idea. I had this vision of where the company could go. With so many people saying I had a brilliant product, how could I walk away?

It would have been very easy at that point to cut our losses. My husband could have said that at any time—but he didn't. I sometimes wonder why.

CHAPTER 6

SWIMMING WITH SHARKS

I HAD MONEY AND AN IDEA. Now it was time to build a team.
So, I started by building a team of moms. One of Jake's friends
came over to play one day, and I got to talking with his mom.
We'll call her Stacy. She worked with her husband, who was a
graphic designer. As we chatted, I told her about my new start-up
and that I'd have to start hiring people soon.

"Oh, that sounds so interesting," she said. "I'd love to do
something like that. Are you taking applications?"

I could feel my heart skip a beat. Was this actually coming
together? I didn't have a formal hiring plan in place yet, so I smiled
and made it up as I went.

"Great! I think we'd love to interview you. I'll have to run it by
a couple people first, but you sound like a qualified candidate!"

By "run it by a couple people," I meant Russell and Vivian,
my friend I first told about the project. I wanted to see what

other people who didn't know her from the kids' school thought about Stacy.

Naturally, I was worried I wouldn't hire the right person. I'd hired people before when I worked my conference job. I'd managed people there too. I'd even stayed friends with some of the people I worked with! But this felt different. It was my own company now, and the position was selling wholesale to retail buyers. I'd never hired anyone for that kind of job.

Vivian, though, had worked in the garment industry for so many years. She'd hired a lot of people. She knew what to look for, the presence of red flags or gold stars. I felt like I needed to have someone who interviewed all the time to sit there and weigh in on what we were doing. After all, there is no shame in asking for help when you *know* someone else has the skills.

So, Vivian came with me to the interview. We all met at a hotel lounge in Hoboken that divided the distance between us. I still felt anxious, but I felt good—like I was about to make some real progress. Vivian, of course, seemed calm and friendly.

We asked Stacy about the work she did with her husband and if she had any sales experience from previous jobs. Back then, we had to do a *lot* of cold calling, so a flair for sales was a must. It was exciting—though I knew there could be challenges that came with hiring someone whose kid attended the same school as mine. During the interview, she seemed very pleasant and flexible. Some of those qualities turned out to be less true than I'd originally thought, but it was ultimately a good move for that point in time.

Stacy was great on the phone. She was a natural at customer service, and the buyers loved her. She was excellent at keeping people engaged, which is hard to do when you're cold calling. We had a script, of course, to make sure we remembered to talk about all the important points. But some people just have the gift of cold calling and some do not.

Stacy used to make some mistakes—like getting the name of the company wrong. In the beginning, she'd accidentally call the company Just Bones Swimwear instead of Just Bones Boardwear. But she had a real warmth about her that drew people in. When she called people, she always seemed so genuine and enthusiastic. She'd laugh a lot. She'd ask about our buyers' lives. It resonated with people. They didn't feel like she was just trying to sell them something. She was a good listener. Even at trade shows, buyers would come in and seek her out. They liked her on the phone and wanted to meet her in person.

For all the good things Stacy brought to the company, there were uncomfortable moments too.

She sent us an invitation to her son's bar mitzvah, around eight weeks in advance. We RSVP'd early on, knowing she'd feel slighted if we didn't go, which could have become a major issue at work. But it turned out that on that same day, one of my best friends from prep school planned to get married. He'd been with his partner for years, and same-sex marriage had just been legalized. My friend didn't send the wedding invitation much in advance, and we'd already RSVP'd to the bar mitzvah. Even worse, I found out that I was the only high school friend invited to the wedding. I desperately wanted to go to his wedding, but I knew if I didn't go to the bar mitzvah there would be repercussions. Dreading my friend's disappointment, and the fun I would miss, I skipped my first gay wedding bash. I didn't know it then, but awkward invitations and possible social fallout would be the least of my worries with Stacy. But I'll return to all that drama later.

About a month before the accident, I got a call from a woman, Jayme Bohn, a production and costume designer, asking if she could use our adjustable waist boardshorts for product placement in a new movie that was in the works for the Syfy Channel. She was looking for swimwear that would fit the younger cast members. She really liked the idea of having an adjustable waist—it meant fewer alterations and less work for the on-set seamstress.

Of course, I agreed. This sounded like an amazing opportunity!

The movie, an original production by SyFy, was called *Ghost Shark*. In the era of *Sharknado*, it was as ridiculous and amusing as the name suggests. In the movie, a couple of men in a fishing town kill a great white shark. To their horror, they discover the beast's ghost would seek revenge. The ghost shark kills the fishermen and begins its reign of terror. A group of teenagers, consisting of the fishermen's two daughters and their friends, see the ghost shark in action and try to warn the town, but of course—at first—no one believes them.

In its ghostly form, the shark is able to attack in *any* body of water, from the ocean to the pool to the bath to the rain. With the help of a mysterious lighthouse keeper, the teens gather the clues they need to defeat the bloodthirsty specter.

When the movie came out, Russell, the kids, and I all gathered around the television to watch. Russell and I shared a bottle of wine, and we all munched on popcorn as we tried to spot the boardshorts on screen. We burst into fits of laughter when we realized that nearly every character who wore our boardshorts ended up getting killed by the ghost shark.

Even more thrilling, *Ghost Shark* aired during the Discovery Channel's annual Shark Week. Shark Week is one of the longest running and continuously popular events in network TV history.

It aims to entertain and educate—mixing ridiculous movies such as *Ghost Shark*, classics such as *Jaws*, and educational programs that teach about the important roles sharks play in the oceans' ecosystems.

In 2018, Shark Week nabbed nearly 35 million total viewers, according to *Forbes*. That's no small accomplishment for sharks—or for us![1]

CHAPTER 7

OPPORTUNITY KNOCKS

I N SPRING OF 2011, AND six months after my attorney filed the trademark and logo for Just Bones Boardwear, someone tried to block me from using our brand name and logo! My attorney had received a notice of opposition.

Our products essentially had nothing in common, but the guy who filed the opposition had a reputation for being litigious. He would oppose any mark with the word "bone" or "bones" in it.

I couldn't believe the lawyers I had retained didn't give me a heads up on this. Once I started doing some research, I found he had a long history of going after other businesses, small, and large, even if it made no sense to do so.

Despite the lawsuit looming, we planned to go to West Palm Beach with the boys and two of their friends over Spring Break. My family saw the chance to relax and have a nice vacation. I saw a business opportunity. Florida would be an incredible market to break into. There were endless streams of tourists looking to buy boardshorts and no shortage of locals looking for the same. I had to try.

So, I took some samples with me. I thought maybe I'd meet some buyers and could get them to be retail customers. I cold called stores that seemed to be in tourist-heavy locations. I was able to see some places in Boca Raton, Palm Beach, and Parkland before I decided to try to get in touch with a sales rep in a showroom at the Miami International Merchandise Mart, a wholesale and retail marketplace featuring product lines in multiple categories.

"Do you know about the SwimShow?" he asked.

"No, I don't think I do…. What is it?" I replied.

"It's the biggest trade show in Florida. It's an international swimwear show in July. You should check it out," he said.

July? It was April then, so there were only a few months in between. I Googled the show. There wasn't much about the event available online unless you were already an exhibitor, so I decided to call the main office to learn more. I felt butterflies in my stomach and didn't know what to expect. To gather my thoughts, I stepped outside before I made the call to be near the pool. There was just something about being outside near the water—whether it was the pool or the ocean—that calmed me. Maybe it's because I grew up in Miami, or maybe it's because I'm a water sign, but being near water never failed to help.

As I paced back and forth near the pool, I finally dialed the number.

"Hi, my name is Jennifer, and I'd like to learn more about the SwimShow. I have some new boardshorts I'm hoping to display," I said. I wanted to sound confident, but not overly, so I could only trust I struck the right balance.

"Oh sure, you can come by our office, bring your samples, and meet with us," said the voice on the other end of the line.

Was this really happening?

"Great! I'll be there," I said.

I collected my new samples and hung them on dark wooden hangers. They were the kind with big, sturdy clips you'd hang pants up with. They looked like they belonged in a custom walk-in closet or designer clothing store. I thought this might be the only way I could get the brand in front of the right eyes so I wanted to do what I could to make the boardshorts look high-end.

When I got to the office, I gingerly laid out the product I'd spent so many hours working to perfect. It was in their hands now. Judy Stein, the executive director of the SwimShow, looked over the boardshorts.

She liked them. No—she loved them!

She even commented on the hangers! So many people, she told me, would simply throw their samples out on the table without thinking anything of their presentation.

"We'd love to have you exhibit this July," she said. "We've already closed our contracts for the show this year, but we'll give you a booth if you sign up right now."

Naturally, I signed up on the spot.

I was all set to be in my first trade show! Now I just had to figure out how to pull that off in three months.

CHAPTER 8

ROAD WARRIOR

ONE OF MY CHILDHOOD FRIENDS came to help me set up for the trade show at the Miami Beach Convention Center. The venue was enormous, stretching for blocks along Convention Center Drive. My friend and I referred to the map provided to track down the exhibitor entrance around the side of the building, where the truck bays were. Before we were allowed onto the showroom floor, we had to check in at registration. Judy Stein seemed thrilled to see me and gave me a huge welcome as I retrieved our exhibitor badges. After searching the countless numbered aisles, we finally located my booth in the kids' section of the show. It was so exciting to see the Just Bones Boardwear logo imprinted on a huge sign across the top of the booth. Luckily, all the boxes I shipped had arrived and were stacked inside of the booth. Some were in better shape than others, but they made it there and nothing was damaged. Back then, I had no idea what I really needed to make a booth pop. At that moment, I was glad I made the decision to have black walls instead of plain white. We started by hanging up all the boardshorts and organizing them by size. We began with boys' size 5 on the top hang bars and finished with boys' size 20 on the bottom hang bars. I merchandised all the boardshort sizes by prints and colorways, like you would find shopping in a store. I decided to fill in a few spaces with our white logo Just Bones Boardwear tees. Next, I hung the few lifestyle posters I had printed with photos I took of Jake and Josh wearing the new boardshorts across the back wall.

Once that was done, I thought we'd be set! But the booth looked *so* empty compared to other booths around us. It wasn't just the limited product—back then, I only had boys' boardshorts. I didn't have decorations or something to make my booth stand out in the sea of exhibitors. Some booths had fancy couches, plush chairs with ottomans, even mini fridges and tropical plants that made their booths look so inviting for buyers to hang out in. Apparently, I needed those! But this was now the eleventh hour. A few of the big-name brands had small mansions as booths, and you could not even see inside of them. Entry was as exclusive as nightclubs.

I ran out with my friend to buy a rug and other décor to make my space look more beachy. We found a cute area rug that would add that rustic beach vibe. I spotted some fun aqua directors' chairs with a white wood finish. Now *these* would add some vibrant color to the booth! Lastly, I picked up a cool, used surfboard from a surf shop at Nikki Beach to put in the corner of the booth. It was the perfect color teal with painted skulls scattered across the deck. I bought some other baubles to make the place look lively and inviting, taking cues from neighboring booths. I added a framed story about how I began the company, along with a bowl of Smarties for the buyers. After all, doesn't everyone enjoy a sweet treat? I heard that research showed eating candy can literally have a positive effect on our mood, and I wanted the buyers to be happy!

Eventually, with two trade shows under my belt, I would order custom wood flooring to make our booth stand out from all the carpeted booths. It was precisely what I needed for that beach life vibe. But it was a huge pain to haul out of the gigantic hard plastic tubes it was shipped in. There were two pieces of flooring I needed to place side by side to cover my booth space, which had now doubled, so I needed two heavy shipping tubes to get the flooring from FedEx into my SUV. And getting that temporary wood flooring rolled up and back into the molded tubes was no easy feat at the end of each show. It was a workout even with two people! I didn't hire a custom trade show booth company for some time, therefore we were doing some of the manual labor ourselves. But I wasn't afraid of hard work.

When my first buyer at the SwimShow came in, I remember thinking she looked so elegant. She was dressed in flowing white linen resort wear and fashionable leather sandals. Her hair was long and blonde with perfect, beachy waves. Even though she wore makeup, it was effortlessly minimal. She was beautiful, and she knew it. But she was still kind without being affected. She sat down to speak with me and talk about our product. She came in with another woman and said they weren't looking to place a huge order, but they were interested. They had a small boutique on an island in the Bahamas.

At the time, I didn't know anything about Harbor Island, although now I know it's an expensive, exclusive place to go vacation.

"We don't order a lot of anything," she said. "We'll order a few prints in various sizes. What are your minimums?"

I was completely unprepared, since this was the first day at my first trade show, but so happy to get an order. I gave the two women all the information they asked for, they placed their order, and then just seemed to float away.

The minute they left, someone from another booth walked over to me.

"Do you know who that was?" she asked.

"My first buyer!" I replied.

"That was India Hicks!"

"Okay?"

"India Hicks! She's a model. She was one of Princess Diana's bridesmaids and is a relative of the British royal family. She's really famous," she said.

What?! A famous person came by, and I didn't even realize it?

Her business partner had signed the purchase order, so I didn't manage to get an autograph, but she was my client for many years after that. I adored how she nonchalantly snacked on the Smarties I had out in the bowl.

To top it off, the SwimShow had its own live fashion show. Each exhibitor was allowed one swimwear or cover-up piece in the show. Organizers asked us to send them three pieces in advance we liked the most, then they chose which piece went out on the runway. Everything at the SwimShow is juried. There were more than 500 exhibitors, so the fashion show was set to be an evening event for buyers and exhibitors at the end of the second day, cocktail party and all.

We made sure to get good seats. We sat four rows back from the stage—considering how many people attended, we were pretty close!

Most of it felt like a Victoria's Secret event. Gorgeous models strutted down the stage wearing a wide array of bikinis, cover-ups, and nude high heels. Every time a male model walked out, my heart jumped up in my throat. Were those my boardshorts?

Finally, a teenage boy with long blond hair, rocking the surfer look, walked out wearing Just Bones Boardwear. My boardshorts were on a model! On a runway! He did one quick lap, and it was over in a minute. It was like a rollercoaster. There was all this buildup, and then it was over—free fall to nothing. We sat through the rest of the show and admired all the other swimwear designs.

For all the fun and excitement, I learned some hard lessons too.

My booth was directly across from a couple women selling girls' bikinis. It was pink and pretty and a totally opposite style to my boardshorts. I got along with those two women well. We were all there for our first trade show and became friendly. One of them was pregnant, but she hadn't started showing and wasn't publicizing her condition.

Another couple of women were selling kids' swimwear at a corner booth nearby. Their line was more volley shorts than classic boardshorts—the kind I used to shop for. We didn't talk a great deal, but I noticed one day that the two women left about 15 minutes early, before the show ended. I didn't give it much thought until another woman walked up to the now empty booth, crouched under the skirted table, and pulled out a plastic file box filled with a bunch of paperwork.

I made eye contact with the women at the girls' bikini booth as if to ask, *She isn't supposed to be doing that, is she?*

This mysterious woman heaved the big box up and started walking down the aisle toward the trade show exit sign. Suddenly, the pregnant woman took off running after the thief in her wedges, yelling for security. I ran over to the deserted corner booth to search for a phone number for the women who had left.

Security came and stopped the thief, and I finally got the women from the empty booth on the phone. They had walked to a hotel bar for happy hour drinks. They ran back immediately, arriving sweaty and disheveled.

In that moment, we felt like heroes. We'd saved the day!

The women working the corner show booth were questioned by police, who decided it was good old-fashioned corporate espionage. The thief ended up spending the night in jail.

By the next day, the two who ran the corner booth were chatting with me regularly and complimenting me on my boardshorts. It seemed like they wanted to be friends. They asked me if they could purchase a couple of my boardshorts because they absolutely loved them and they both had boys. The trade show had a strict policy about selling your samples at the end of the show, but I figured since I wasn't technically *selling all my sample boardshorts* to customers, it would be okay.

Besides, I was trying to network in a cutthroat industry, and it was *only two pairs*. What was the harm in that?

Well, the joke was on me.

Two shows later, the corner booth women were displaying a new design very similar to mine, complete with skulls. I was so mad at myself. I'd been going through all this trouble, and spending tons of money, to protect my product with a patent, and all of my intellectual property, and then I did this! They'd pretended to be my friends, but they were two-faced liars. They tried to do exactly what that thief tried to do! They honestly never even thanked the three of us for saving their butts.

From that moment on, I promised myself I wouldn't be so naïve again. I'd heard of one exhibitor in Vegas having 20 sample garments go missing one night, so I started to lock up all my products every day when shows ended. I got heavy-duty zippered canvas garment bags with a lock clip that went over the hangers, which I could secure with a zip tie. If someone truly wanted to, they could cut through the zip tie, but then I'd know someone tampered with it. It took an extra 10 minutes to close up each night, but it was worth it. Many booths used these type of garment bags, or other ways to lock up, but I was surprised how many simply threw tablecloths or sheets over their products each night before leaving.

I learned I had to keep my eyes peeled for manufacturers posing as buyers looking to scope out the competition too. So many manufacturers come and scout out the trade shows, even though they aren't supposed to.

It was such a whirlwind experience. From designing the boardshort to receiving my first samples to getting it into stores to exhibiting at trade shows—I couldn't believe how far I'd already come.

At that first trade show, a couple women I met told me they were from the Surf Expo. They asked me if I wanted to exhibit at their trade show in September in Orlando. It sounded amazing, so I quickly looked it up online. I committed to that show the very next day because they emailed me a contract, but this time I only had two months to prepare!

That night, I breathed my first sigh of relief. I was getting sales! Russell had taken a chance and believed in my idea, and I wasn't letting him down. The SwimShow now a success, I returned home.

While the boys were busy with baseball, I decided to see what other sales I could close. I called a bunch of stores in the Cape Cod area in Massachusetts and scheduled appointments to show them our product. I promised myself I'd take whatever I could get. The road trip was only a little over six hours, and I had done it before when the kids went to summer camp on the Cape. By now, I had received my first delivery from the factory in China and I had box upon box of boardshorts piled up in our garage. So, I neatly packed up an assortment of boardshorts in different prints and sizes into plastic bins and loaded them into my SUV. I'd be gone for a few days, but I wasn't worried since most of it was during the weekend.

Some of the other baseball moms, however, were surprised.

"You're just going to get in the car by yourself and drive to Cape Cod? Without your husband or a girlfriend?" one mom asked.

"Well, yeah," I said. "It's a sales trip. No one wants to come merely to sit in the car as I drive around and talk to buyers."

She, and many others, looked at me like I was crazy! But actually, it wasn't a big deal.

I managed to set up about 10 appointments between Cape Cod, Martha's Vineyard, and Nantucket. I would have to take a ferry over to Martha's Vineyard and Nantucket for my appointments, so I'd arranged ahead for that, along with a delightful bed-and-breakfast in Edgartown to stay the night on Martha's Vineyard. These were both popular summer vacation spots, and it was already growing busy in May.

For each meeting, I walked in with my boardshorts prepped and pressed. I wanted to make a good impression. Then I explained how my adjustable waist boardshorts were a brand-new concept—how I would have loved to buy a pair myself before I invented them because of my sons.

I came back with six new accounts after that trip, some of which are still customers. I felt fantastic. People had doubted me, and now I was proving that all the hard work and the long hours, combined with putting myself out there, were finally paying off. To this day, as we are still selling to some of these retail stores, I stay in touch with the buyers. It's still a wonderful feeling nearly a decade later because they all took a chance on me when we were an unknown brand, not knowing how our product would sell to their customers.

Retail store names are a funny thing, especially for swimwear. When you think of a good one, you want to keep it. Over the years, I've seen many interesting names—some make me a little envious, some make me laugh, and some make me blush.

Some names can be mistaken for awkward sexual innuendos or even adult stores. That kind of thing can often get a laugh, especially from those vacationing at resorts. But once, I think it actually caused us a shipment issue!

One of our early retail customers owns and runs a store called Wetter or Not. She ordered boardshorts from us at a show in the fall before the summer season was set to begin. Her store is in The Hamptons, a trendy seaside resort on New York's Long Island that's about a two-hour drive from us. But she never received her delivery! We called FedEx over and over, asking where the shipment was, but they kept telling us they didn't know and they couldn't find it.

We sent the buyer another box of product at our expense so she could unpack and merchandise before the season started, but we still needed to hunt down our missing boardshorts so that we didn't lose money. Plus, we had other orders to fulfill with those missing boardshorts!

About two or three weeks later, we received a call from FedEx. They had found our box at a warehouse about halfway between us and our buyer. Somehow, the top of the box had been ripped off so no one could find the store's address or our company's return address. Anyone who knows me also knows I don't mess around when it comes to taping up my boxes. I usually layer the tape on thick with at least three strips going one way and three strips going the other to keep the product properly sealed.

Russell, always one to give people the benefit of the doubt, said maybe the forklift somehow ripped off the box top. But that hasn't happened before or since. And even if it had, they'd still have the addresses somewhere in their system. Fortunately, FedEx figured out the box belonged to us from our boardshort hang tags and called us.

I suspect what really happened was that some fool who was a total pervert thought the contents of the box were going to an adult store. I think they put it aside, opened it up, and quickly realized it had nothing to do with what he was hoping for. I'm guessing he was so embarrassed by the discovery he tossed the top of the box and didn't ever say a word about it.

CHAPTER 9

THE DAY MY LIFE CHANGED

U NTIL THE ACCIDENT, I'D BEEN spinning all kinds of plates in the air. It was a delicate balance, and I worked hard not to drop any. But when the car slammed me to the ground, all those plates came crashing down around me like delicate china.

When the ambulance came, I wasn't yet worried about the pain in my head or my shoulder because I was still in shock. Instead, I was freaking out about being strapped down to the spinal board they were starting to load me on.

I kept telling the paramedics, through tears, that I was claustrophobic and they couldn't strap my arms down. I begged them for a sedative to calm me down. But they told me I could not have any medication before I was evaluated at the hospital. Jake was holding my hand tightly. He could see the fear in my eyes. He wanted to ride in the ambulance with me, but the paramedics said he couldn't because, being under eighteen, he wasn't old enough.

So, I was loaded into the ambulance alone and afraid. Russell had the boys and his car in Millburn, and they followed the ambulance to the hospital. It felt like the longest ride of my life—one that would never end.

We were reunited in the ER at the trauma hospital. I asked Russell to get the boys out of there, knowing it could be hours of them waiting around. He called their friends' mothers, and along with their two best friends, they rushed to pick up Josh and Jake. Everyone wanted the details on how I was doing. News of the accident was spreading fast.

I waited *hours* for a CAT scan machine, although I had been evaluated by an ER doctor and my head was still bleeding. There were a couple people ahead of me—one with a serious gunshot wound and another who'd been impaled. All I wanted was to be freed from the neck collar and taken off that spinal board. It felt as though I was trapped, imprisoned in a straitjacket. I was not allowed to use the bathroom or have anything to drink or eat. I wondered what my sons were doing. How were they? Were they alright? I wanted to hug them both and tell them I would be okay. This was not how I planned this day to end. We were supposed to be having fun planning their big party after the temple service.

Russell called the party planner, told her what had happened, and canceled our meeting for the following day. Eventually, after they took me in for the CAT scan, they wheeled me back to wait for the ER doctor again. Thankfully, the scan results showed I had no broken bones and my skull was not fractured.

But I did have a severe concussion, a bone contusion on my right hip where the car struck me, road rash on my body and face, and my shoulder required a sling. I also needed 15 staples to close my head wound, which were administered without the aid of a lidocaine injection. The staff was overwhelmed and advised me I'd have to wait 45 minutes more if I received lidocaine. I wasn't thinking clearly, so I let them go ahead with the staples sans medication. A while after the accident, I'd had a very specific brain MRI for my lawsuit, and the doctors found I had suffered a brain bleed, which was not discovered during the ER visit. Thank goodness nothing terrible happened overnight, since they discharged me hours later after tending to my vital wounds. I also sustained a traumatic brain injury (TBI)—but more on that later.

Russell and my friend still had to worry about driving my car back from the municipal lot, getting the boys home, and bringing in some dinner. It was difficult to eat, but I was hungry since my last meal was breakfast. I showered while Russell took care of everything. I needed to wash all the dried blood off and get it out of my hair. The warm water stung the freshly stapled wound on my scalp and the road rash, but I managed to get through bathing myself. I genuinely wished they had given me the pain medication for my head wound.

My shoulder immediately gave me a lot of trouble and required a trip to an orthopedic surgeon. Even after a cortisone shot, my range of motion was fairly limited, and I suffered daily pain. The orthopedic surgeon sent me for an arthrogram. Unfortunately, even with contrast, it didn't show what my shoulder injury was— slap tear, bicep tendon damage, or rotator cuff tear. He wanted to schedule diagnostic laparoscopic surgery to go in and repair whatever he found was wrong. I was not prepared for exploratory surgery and wanted to at least get a second opinion. I didn't want to go under the knife without some sort of explanation as to what was causing my shoulder pain. In the meantime, he prescribed a prescription compound cream that helped with some of the daily pain.

Before the accident, I was known for cooking up gourmet-style meals every night for my family. I love to cook and never missed an opportunity to make a meal exciting. But that was over, at least for now. I couldn't lift my arm up past 90 degrees, so even blow-drying my hair was difficult. Playing tennis or golf again seemed like a pipe dream. I had trouble stirring a pot of marinara, whisking a vinaigrette, or beating eggs for breakfast. Chopping vegetables or prepping food for dinner was no easy task, and it all aggravated my shoulder. It would angrily throb in pain.

But beyond just physically making the meal, I'd always been the one to plan dinners. If I didn't cook, I still decided where we would go out for dinner or bring food in from. But now with my traumatic brain injury, I was so mentally burnt out by the end of the day, that there were days I could not even decide what type of cuisine we should order. My family would ask, "Do you want Italian? Mexican? Chinese?" I couldn't answer! I was just so exhausted after only working a few hours that my brain literally shut down. It was like the curtain falling at the end of a show or a computer shutting down. I simply ran out of juice. I felt like a nap instead of food. With three people staring at me and throwing suggestions simultaneously at me about dinner, it felt like birds pecking at my head, and I could not escape.

They got so annoyed with me, but I couldn't make a decision despite their persistence. That's when I started to understand what my cognitive behavioral therapist meant when she said I had a blind injury. I was healing on the outside, but I had a long way to go for my TBI recovery.

I felt guilty. I'd always provided dinner. I was the caretaker, but I couldn't be that person right now. In the moment, it felt like my family were blaming me for being different. But I hadn't asked for this. I never would have chosen this.

My doctors told me it can be hard, even for your close family and friends, to remember something's different when you suffer a traumatic brain injury. I didn't have an injury people could physically see. I wasn't in a wheelchair or using crutches, nor did I have a cast on anywhere. I looked the same as I always looked, but I was a different person right after the accident. They wanted me to be the mom I was before. They never said it out loud, but I could tell that was the expectation. They couldn't wrap their heads around this *new* me. I remember feeling mad at my family then. I was bewildered. How could they be upset with me because I couldn't decide on dinner? I was the victim here!

I've since come to realize that people *do* get angry when those they love get hurt, sick, or injured. They want to be in control and don't know how to deal with it when they aren't and feel helpless. Sometimes they take out that frustration on the people suffering the illness or injury. They don't like that you're more vulnerable now.

The new me was different than the old me. How was it possible to be so afraid?! When I was younger and carefree before I had kids, I was certified to scuba dive, went flying in single-engine planes and would go parasailing. For years after the accident, I was terrified whenever someone else drove. I would cling to the door handle for dear life, my heart racing with fear and panic. There were times when I would tell my husband he had to stop so I could get out of the car, my PTSD was so out of control.

My family were often frustrated with me. Why couldn't I just sit in the car for a short ride to the restaurant down the road? It caused a lot of turmoil. They couldn't understand how upset and scared I was. I truly felt as if I was going to die from riding in the car, despite the fact that I had been a pedestrian in the accident.

No amount of therapy I went to could fix it. I often woke up in the middle of the night, drenched in sweat after another nightmare about the accident.

Loud noises made me jump out of my skin.

No matter how many times I tried to explain it to my family, they didn't understand why I couldn't control how I felt internally. I couldn't *not* be afraid. I couldn't logically think my way out of this fear. It's the same as telling someone not to be scared of dogs—you don't know what happened to them in the past. If a dog bit them, they can't simply decide not to be afraid.

For a long time, I didn't feel safe. I couldn't even drive through Millburn for a few years, let alone walk near that intersection. If we *had* to make a trip that could not avoid the town, I'd close my eyes until we arrived at our destination.

The accident had deep impacts on my family too. I wanted us all to go to therapy, but I couldn't force two 13-year-old boys to do that. So, we endured a lot of disruption and discord. I needed their help now to do the things I used to do. I asked them to decide in advance what they'd want for dinner. That helped, to a degree, take the guesswork out of what they wanted that night. It also helped me plan the grocery list more efficiently.

In a perfect world, I would have loved to have a system we followed to a T—that really would have helped me. But you can't actually put life into a calendar like that. Life isn't that simple, and it's impossible to get people on the same page every time.

We'd have to adjust.

I came to understand that the boys likely suffered from post-traumatic stress disorder, or PTSD, in the aftermath of the accident as well. They saw their mom bleeding in the street and taken away by an ambulance, not knowing what would happen. Russell wondered if I would live or die, he later told me. I know now that even witnessing a traumatic event like that can cause PTSD, whether that takes the form of flashbacks, nightmares, anxiety, or more.

According to the Mayo Clinic, with time and good self-care, most people are eventually able to adjust even after going through something traumatic, but PTSD can interfere with that.[2] The Mayo Clinic groups PTSD symptoms into four types: "intrusive memories, avoidance, negative changes in thinking and mood, and changes in physical and emotional reactions."[3]

Intrusive memories may look like reoccurring, upsetting memories of the event, flashbacks, upsetting dreams, or extreme reactions to things that remind you of what happened.

Avoidance may look like working to avoid thinking about or talking about what happened or avoiding places or people that trigger memories.

Negative changes in thinking and mood may look like feeling hopeless about the future, experiencing memory problems, having a hard time maintaining relationships, and more.

But some of it can also look like the struggles of young adulthood, like irritability, angry outbursts, trouble sleeping and concentrating, and self-destructive behaviors like driving too fast or drinking too much.[4]

It took time for us all to figure it out. There were some bumps in the road, but we stuck together.

Eventually, I found a good support system outside of my family. I did lots of outpatient therapy—physical, occupational, vestibular, and cognitive behavioral—at two hospitals, however it didn't help with all of my psychological needs. We tried a larger support group at Kessler Rehabilitation Center a few times, but to no avail. There were too many different people with too many diverse conditions to get anything constructive done. People came in with all kinds of brain injuries and types of medical problems. Some were minor compared to mine; some were much worse. The lady running this group told me she had someone in mind who had similar issues to me that she thought would be good for me to talk to.

She passed my phone number along to this woman, who also lived locally. She was part of a much smaller support group, but they had already been meeting together for some time and unfortunately it was too late for me to join. She turned out to be a wonderful connection. She hadn't been in a car accident, but she also had a traumatic brain injury and PTSD. She was so easy to talk to. She *understood* me. She understood how hard it was to look completely ordinary while struggling with some major internal changes.

We got coffee together at least once a month at a local coffee joint since we tended to avoid crowded Starbucks. We'd call and text each other quite often as well. At times, I would see people I knew from the kids' school or locally, and I could see the question in their eyes, *Who is this older woman Jennifer is hanging out with lately?* Of course, this was purely their endless desire for juicy morsels of gossip. For that reason, I was always careful to get a corner table away from prying ears so we could speak privately.

Eventually, we went out with our husbands. It was so nice to have someone around who truly understood and got me, no judgment.

For anyone who experiences a major trauma, whatever it is, it's important to have people around you who you can talk to. I don't think anyone can manage the aftermath of trauma well by themselves. Having people you trust whom you can share your story with is what gets you through the rough patches—and there will be rough patches.

I learned you can't only talk to your friends about it all the time. Sure, your friends want to be there for you, but if that's all you talk about with them, it can strain the relationship.

I decided then that people are either victims or survivors. I don't think everyone can get through a trauma the same way, but it's so important to find what works. If you don't figure out how to keep going, it will swallow you up.

By *survivor*, I don't mean you have to become a hardened, unforgiving person. I'm still a very sensitive, giving, and compassionate person. I just made the decision not to let my experience control my life. That doesn't mean that every day is a picnic either. It simply means I'm determined to do the best I can every day.

Determined to keep moving forward, I went back to work as soon as I could. That was my way of dealing with everything and coping with the accident. It was a welcomed distraction. But during this time, I couldn't pack or lift boxes, and I couldn't go see customers. For what felt like the first time in my life, I had to rely heavily on others to do things for me.

The trade shows were especially challenging. When we set up the booth, we'd have to steam the garments to make them look presentable, considering they were wrinkled by the time we took them out from being packed up and shipped. Previously, I always helped with the steaming, but when my shoulder was injured, it was difficult to do. Moving my arm up and down repeatedly, while holding something for that long, was impossible. Yet, even though everyone knew what had happened to me, my team of moms didn't volunteer to do it for me and actually expected my help. In fact, they kind of scoffed at the idea that I wasn't helping. But it wasn't as if I was asking them to do something I wasn't willing to do myself—I just physically couldn't do it.

CHAPTER 10

MY DOCTORS AND DANCE CARD

B EFORE THE ACCIDENT, OUR SOCIAL calendar was always booked. I used to go out with people because they were my husband's friends or we wanted to keep up with some acquaintances. Truthfully, I tolerated a lot of people I didn't like all that much. I think most of us do.

But after the accident, I realized life is way too short for this. I didn't want to waste my time going out with people I didn't want to be with. That included some people I used to consider my friends.

It came to a head for me at a friend's 50th birthday party about a year after the accident. I'd been looking forward to this party. I felt better than I had in a long time, and I was ready to get out and mingle.

We'd been there maybe 10 minutes when we spotted our birthday friend. As we were about to say hello, another couple cut in. The wife began speaking really fast and excitedly.

"Jennifer, did you hear? A man got hit by a car in the same crosswalk you did. But guess what—he refused medical attention, and he died that night from a head injury. Can you believe it?"

It was simply an interesting piece of gossip to her. She could not wait to tell me the news. Back then, I got extremely upset when people talked about car accidents. It brought me right back to the moment that forever changed my life. I made a run to the bathroom, locked myself in a stall, and cried for a few minutes, praying nobody could hear me. It took some effort, but I steadied my breathing and cleaned up my face as much as I could before leaving the bathroom.

Russell met me as soon as I came out.

"I need to go home," I said.

I knew our friends hosting the party would be put out—it was a sit-down dinner at a country club that we'd RSVP'd for—but I needed to get out of there. The woman who made the comment didn't understand why I was so upset, and I didn't have the energy to explain to her how traumatic it had been or how thoughtless her comment was.

When we got home, our kids were surprised.

"You're home already? It's only been half an hour!"

That's all I could take.

As time went on, I started looking at my friendships differently. I wanted to spend more time with people who were thoughtful, genuine friends. If that meant I had fewer people to send holiday cards to, that was fine by me. I started paring down my

Facebook friends, other social media connections, and weekend commitments.

It suddenly occurred to me that life is not a popularity contest. Quantity didn't matter to me anymore. Quality did.

The physical pain was bad enough. But I also had to deal with the headache that was the personal injury lawsuit from the car accident. That lawsuit went on for six years. *Six years.* The fact that the distracted driver hit me when I had the right of way was obvious, and there were multiple eyewitnesses, but the rules for the auto insurance settlement were very stringent. The insurance company could send me to whatever doctor they deemed necessary for their case, and I was required to go. Let's just say the doctors who work for insurance companies aren't the kinds of doctors you want to go to for surgery or medical opinions. Their job isn't to be nice to you. Rather, their job is basically to find fault with your claim and discredit you—even if you've just been through horrific physical trauma.

The local orthopedist the insurance company sent me to didn't think my injuries were that bad, and he tried to convince *me* of that. Of course he did. He was getting paid to do so. So, why did a top sports medicine surgeon at the Hospital for Special Surgery in New York City have to work on three parts of my shoulder during a lengthy surgery?

Every time I went to one of those insurance mandated doctors, I'd leave upset. It would ruin my entire day. Often, I'd have to wait there for two hours just to get seen by the doctor I didn't want to see.

After some visits, I couldn't bring myself to go back to work. It got to the point where I knew if I had one of those independent medical examination (IME) doctor appointments—which I couldn't skip or get out of because the insurance company required it—I just wouldn't plan anything else for the rest of the day.

That went on for six miserable years. Toward the end, I started questioning if my claim was even worth pursuing, but then I would think, *I'm not going to give into them now after all my family has been through! This lady ran me over!*

CHAPTER 11

DOG-EAT-DOG WORLD

O F COURSE, ALL THIS WAS happening on top of the trademark lawsuit. Before I filed for my trademark, I employed a boutique law firm that specialized in intellectual property to do research on the name. The lawyer I hired ran it by one of the partners at the firm, or so she said, and told me she didn't see any problems with filing for Just Bones Boardwear. So, I went ahead with it.

After the opposition was filed, I reviewed the extensive research binder from Thomson Reuters and saw that it was full of cases this business owner filed over the years against people and companies who used the word "bones" in their brand name, trademark, or logo. What was worse was that the law firm had given me that research binder themselves!

What was wrong with that law firm? They advised me it was safe to file! And here was this guy, who'd filed *14 other lawsuits* or oppositions against various companies, now on my case.

I tried to dot my i's and cross my t's. I tried to play nice. I didn't *want* to infringe on anyone else's trademark, and I wasn't trying to rip anyone off. I legitimately came up with the name for my brand based upon a nickname for one of our sons and my love of skulls. A good friend, who is a graphic designer and specializes in branding, worked with me for weeks on the logo. I felt like it was the law firm's fault for telling me it was alright to move forward. On top of that, this guy was being unreasonable.

I felt like I couldn't give up either. I was already selling boardshorts to retailers under my company brand name. What would happen if I suddenly disappeared from the trade show circuit under this brand name? If I gave up, I would have to change the company name, and we would have lost a lot of money. Was it going to make us go broke? No. But who wants to throw away money on a frivolous lawsuit?

The whole thing was absurd and expensive. But we felt there was no alternative than to negotiate a settlement. What we didn't know then was how long this would drag out! The settlement process began *three years* of demands and counteroffers being exchanged between our lawyer and his. That took away from our initial profits and, much like the accident, derailed the trajectory we'd been on.

Once, during day one of the Surf Expo trade show, my lawyer emailed to advise me that my adversary had now filed a lawsuit against me in federal court. He was claiming trademark infringement! I had a feeling he had filed *right at that moment* just to mess with my head on that particular day because his company also had a booth and was exhibiting at Surf Expo.

I was upset, but I wanted to focus on the trade show itself, not the guy trying to undermine me. Then I had an idea.

I had someone working for me go check out the guy's booth to see if there were any similar trademarks, symbols, or designs to ours. They also picked up a trade show brochure at the front desk of Surf Expo, which included a map of the event and all of the booth locations. Our booths were nowhere near each other, and we were also in different show sections!

It was nothing sneaky—everything was available for anyone else at the show to easily see.

I was in the "Swim" section of the show because I was selling boardshorts and apparel. This guy was in the "Skate" section, which was predominately hard goods. We were so different in our brands we were separated by what felt like miles at the trade show.

As I collected my evidence, I felt like a dog with a bone. I wasn't going to give up. How could I when so much out there proved my case?

After the trade show was over, I sent this information to my lawyer so I could prove he was being irrational. No one could get confused between our two brands. And he only used this creepy skeleton image on some T-shirts, hoodies, and skateboard decks after it became popular years ago with stickers. I had now made it my business to know all about his company, which I never heard of growing up in south Florida. His mark certainly didn't look anything like our trendy boardshort logo.

Even though it felt like I kept running face-first into bigger and bigger obstacles, I pushed forward. I didn't hesitate long enough to look at the scope of the problem around me, I just kept going.

I'm glad for that now. If I had looked up and beyond the problem right in front of my face, I think I would have been overwhelmed by the enormity of it all. The only way I could keep going was to put one foot in front of the other.

CHAPTER 12

KILL SWITCH

I T'S DIFFICULT TO ACCOUNT FOR how much the accident changed me. My kids used to come home from school, throw their backpacks on the counter, and grab a snack. Before, I could tune them out until I finished what I was working on. I could simply ignore them as I typed up an important email.

But after the accident, those innocent noises were beyond irritating to me. Everything was suddenly so distracting. Soon, instead of ignoring them, I'd snap.

"Stop talking. I'm in the middle of an email," I'd say.

Even the dogs barking bothered me.

No one was used to me behaving this way. It was an adjustment for everyone—even I didn't understand it.

I found myself having trouble with my balance and vision too. Even though my left eye wasn't physically damaged—like a retina tear—from the accident, I lost some of my peripheral vision. I'd misjudge going through the doorways and would hit my shoulder repeatedly. I'd think I was fine, then I'd whack right into the doorjamb. I was constantly banging into the coffee table, stepping on the dogs, and tripping up the stairs.

After being referred, I went in for neurological testing, hoping for some answers, at the JFK Johnson Rehabilitation Institute in northern New Jersey. During the first appointment, I had a thorough neurological examination, which assesses motor and sensory skills, hearing and speech, vision, coordination, and balance.

On the next visit, I endured a neurological test to determine whether the concussion had had an impact on my brain and its functioning.

Doctors put me in a room for six hours straight. It's legitimately designed to see how much you can handle, how well you can focus, and to test your cognitive functioning.

During one test, I had to read a story, summarize it, and answer questions about it. Math problems, solving puzzles, and pattern recognition were also part of the test. The math portion got to me. It was toward the end of testing, and it almost broke me.

During the session, I sat at a desk and listened to a tape recorder. The voice coming out was monotone and boring, droning on and on. The voice told me whether to add or subtract out loud while spouting off numbers.

Tears ran down my face as I tried to keep up. I was tired. *So tired!*

I thought to myself, *Oh my God, I just can't take this anymore!* But still I tried. I added, subtracted, and did as much backwards math as I could handle.

Somehow, I missed a number, and I wasn't allowed to go back. I found myself falling far behind with no chance to recover.

I wanted to shout, *Stop the effing tape recorder now!* I was so angry I wanted to break it.

When the tests were over, the doctor had some answers.

"Imagine a computer that has too much input entered rapidly," the doctor said. "You feed it too much information too fast, and it can't keep up processing, so it just shuts down or freezes. That's a lot like what's happening to your brain function. If you have too many things going on at once, you can't handle it. It becomes overwhelming at minimum."

I already had an inkling this was true, but that did little to temper my shock. I'd been a high-achieving multitasker my entire life. Would this ever get better?

"You're going to have to change your lifestyle," the doctor said. "You're obviously a Type A person, and you're highly motivated. You could probably do ten things at once before, but you can't do that anymore. We find for Type A people this can be a very dramatic change, and it can be difficult to adjust. It'll be important to learn to do one task at a time. Don't let yourself get upset or frustrated at that—it's your new normal. You have a processing disorder from the traumatic brain injury."

Well, that explained why I blew up on my kids. But how in the world was I going to adjust my entire life? I'd always been busy. I liked having a million things to do. This was the beginning of a long journey.

CHAPTER 13

DOWNTOWN SPEEDWAY

A ROUND THE TIME I WAS supervising my first professional photo shoot on the beach in The Hamptons—before my accident—a Millburn High School student was hospitalized after being hit by a car on May 8, 2012.[5]

I didn't hear about it then, but *The Item of Millburn and Short Hills* wrote about it. The student was on her way to work on a media project for school when she crossed the street and was hit. When police officers arrived to help, they worked to brace her neck and spine. They even had to do CPR to keep her heart beating.[6]

In this particular incident, police didn't bring charges against the driver, since the girl and her friends were crossing the road at an angle and the visibility in the area was limited.[7] In a July 12, 2012, editorial, *The Item* called on the town to take action on what locals came to know as the "downtown racecourse" after *another* teenage girl was hit by a car crossing the road. This accident caught the attention of the editorial board for happening in an area between Spring Street and Main Street that lacked a safe crossing area.[8]

The Item noted that local officials then started exploring what options were available to keep people safe, from barriers to angled parking to additional lighting.[9]

I can't help but wonder if the township had taken action sooner whether my own accident could have been avoided altogether.

In August of 2012—a month before my accident—township officials had talked about the traffic issue at length as they discussed the construction of a new supermarket in the area. Residents worried the addition would make a bad traffic spot even worse. Township engineers even agreed then that traffic was a major problem, with accidents happening between cars and pedestrians and with trucks having a hard time turning because Millburn Avenue wasn't a 90-degree angle. Residents questioned the wisdom of bringing large trucks in and out of a space so close to Millburn High School and a local church—especially since the town already had issues with people getting hit by cars.[10]

Then, of course, came *The Item*'s story about my accident at the intersection of Essex and Main Street in the September 20, 2012, issue. The woman who hit me was cited with careless driving and failing to yield to a pedestrian that day.[11]

I remember feeling appalled that she didn't have her license taken away. How did it not at least get suspended? She hadn't been drunk, but she didn't see me. Clearly, she was looking at something else than where she was driving.

More than six months before my accident, the Township Committee acknowledged there was an issue with speed in town. The town briefly installed speed bumps before having them removed, according to *The Item*.[12]

After my accident, the problem persisted for years.

People often wrote letters to the editor, calling for people to stop speeding. In the June 12, 2014, issue, one woman wrote that she witnessed two cars gunning their engines and speeding through the center of town.[13]

It was crazy to me that so many people could ignore this problem. It was dangerous. It was reckless. I couldn't help but wonder how many more people had to get seriously hurt, or maybe even killed, before something significant was done to address the problem.

CHAPTER 14

COMING APART AT THE SEAMS

S TACY, ONE OF MY FIRST hires, was the first person I ever fired. For a while, I felt like things weren't working out. For example, there were multiple times that she wasn't able to make it to trade shows.

One time, it was a family emergency. Her daughter had been selling Cutco knives and somehow cut her arm severely, so Stacy had to stay home because her daughter needed emergency nerve surgery. That obviously made sense, but it was one excuse of many. She'd run into the city for her mother anytime she called, yet bailed when I needed her help because some other family member needed her "more."

During the first trade show after my accident, I experienced many classic PTSD symptoms. It was Surf Expo, and there were so many people and so much going on at one time. I was having a really rough time. The doctors told me I'd have trouble processing so much at once, and I knew I was going against their recommendations by being at the trade show in the first place, but I felt like I *had* to be there. I didn't realize how much it was going to affect my performance.

Stacy had a bad habit of interrupting me—one I didn't actually notice until after the accident. When I'd talk to people coming up to our booth, I'd give them my spiel and talk about the boardshorts. It was somewhat of a script I'd say each time to make sure I covered all of my bullet points.

She'd often interrupt me during my script, thinking she was helping me. But after my accident, it genuinely bothered me. I couldn't find my way back to where she got me off track. I got more frustrated than I would have previously.

I often put my hand up to motion for her to stop talking without even thinking. It became like my shield to protect myself from her interruptions. But she got angry that I was doing it. My hand became a stop sign.

Stacy knew about the accident and knew how it had affected me, but she just couldn't be empathetic about it. She insisted I was being insulting and demeaning. Even if I explained I wasn't doing it on purpose, that I lost my train of thought when she interrupted me, she couldn't understand my point of view.

No matter what angle I came from or how I tried to explain it, she had no room for compassion. To me, she came off like: "I get it; you got hit by a car, but you still can't be rude to me. I came to the trade show *to help you.*"

What was I supposed to do about something I couldn't control?

A fabrication about a migraine was the final straw.

Stacy said she'd come help me pack for a trade show after I had my shoulder surgery, but she didn't show up. She told me on a text that she bailed because of a terrible migraine. I had to call her to finalize a couple details.

"Hey, Stacy, I noticed you haven't canceled your hotel room for Orlando yet," I said. "I went ahead and canceled it for you, but was there a reason you didn't do it?"

I was already annoyed because she was a no-show, but she almost cost us quite a bit of money for that room too.

"Oh, hey, Jen.... I can't talk right now," she said breathlessly. "I'm getting ready to go to Jeff's company Christmas party."

I guess that migraine got better in record time.

It was a short conversation. I didn't confront her then, but I did the next time I saw her at work. But instead of being apologetic or just being plain honest, she got mad and defensive when I called her out on it. Rather than saying, "You know what, I should have approached this differently," she simply blew up.

Then things got even worse between us. We reached the point of no return in our working relationship. We needed to part ways. So, I told her that unfortunately it wasn't going to work out anymore.

Stacy got very angry with me, and we parted on bad terms. I still ran into her at various school functions or games, and it was uncomfortable for a long time. She'd say hello to Russell but not to me. It was as if I was invisible. Eventually, by the time the boys got to high school, she'd mellowed out and started being nicer to me.

Having to fire Stacy felt like just another strike against me. Just Bones Boardwear had been on an amazing trajectory. We'd been going up and up and up—and then, all of a sudden, there was so much stuff crashing down on me that was outside of my control. I felt my entire world caving in around me.

After that trade show, my doctors told me I couldn't work the long, 10- or more-hour days that trade shows often required anymore. I had to scale back.

But how could I do that when my business needed me to succeed?

As I packed everything up, alone, it hit me. I was at my lowest. It was so hard to carry on by myself, and I didn't have loyal people I could count on to be there when I needed them. For a moment I just stopped and let hot tears spill out. I wondered if I could really keep doing this. My doctors told me to slow down, and I didn't listen. Lawsuits weighed me down like anchors I couldn't shake. We'd been doing well. If that stupid car hadn't hit me, I wouldn't be here like this. That woman behind the wheel had no idea what kind of impact she'd had on me, my business, and everyone in my life.

Was I up for this? Even at my lowest point, I never considered giving up. I had a healthy fear of failure, but there was no way I was going down without a fight. It wasn't in my nature. So, I packed everything up. I loaded up the car. And I headed out to fight another day.

CHAPTER 15

SOCIAL MEDIA MANIA

AFTER I LET STACY GO, I knew things had to change. The business had outgrown the team of moms I hired in the beginning. It was time to bring in some professionals who could commit to the work—preferably ones I didn't have to keep seeing at basketball games if things didn't work out.

Russell saw I couldn't manage it all by myself anymore. That wasn't purely because of the accident—the business was growing enough that I needed help with accounts payable, accounts receivable, inventory control, and warehousing issues that I didn't know as much about as he did.

One day, Russell asked me if I wanted him to come help with the business. He had the knowledge and the expertise to handle what I couldn't, so I said yes. He couldn't play golf year-round, after all—his brain would rot!

At that point, I knew it was time to get an office. Russell and I couldn't both be working from home. Everyone would get exasperated with me and all my paperwork, swimwear designs, and Pantone books sprawled out all over the kitchen counters. I asked one of my half-sisters who was in real estate if she knew of anyone who could help us get an office. Luckily, she did! The place we settled on was reasonably priced and in a good location in town, right across the street from the train station.

It was an older brick building, one you could tell had been repainted, with two floors. We shared the space with several other businesses. Though the entire building could use a facelift, it was a good spot. I was beyond excited to have my very first corporate office complete with custom building signage! In addition, the building was right next to a pizza place and a diner.

Inside, the office felt a little dreary, so I had the place repainted. Once the lifeless beige had been replaced with a light blue and we got some new carpet in there, it felt like a much nicer space. It wasn't anything fancy—we only had three little offices, a reception area, and a bathroom—but to have that space made it feel like we were genuinely growing.

Once, at a trade show in Vegas, a man came up to us, interested in Just Bones Boardwear because he saw our signage every day while he waited for the Millburn train to New York. He owned one of the first businesses that was interested in licensing my patents. It ultimately didn't work out with his business, but it was exciting to see what kind of connections we were making, even back then.

Part of me wondered if, in reality, I could spend that much time with my husband. Would we drive each other completely crazy? Would we get annoyed with each other? There were a couple small things that came up, like how he hated it when I asked him to tell the employees to do things if he didn't completely understand what I was talking about—like Photoshop with vector images or use social media tags—or when he didn't understand why it was important for me to know about his appointments while I was making a weekly schedule. But we worked together surprisingly well—especially since I made sure that his office was down the hall and not right next to mine!

When I designed my collections, I created new names and style numbers for all the boardshorts and bikinis. This was for our factory production, inventory control, and the retail buyers for when they placed orders. When Russell went to digitize all the inventory, he would tell me to give him the part numbers so he could put them into the computer. I'd reply, "Oh my *GOD*, Russell, this is fashion! It's a style number, not a part number!" He was so accustomed to dealing with part numbers in his former manufacturing life that he could not wrap his head around fashion jargon.

But he knew how to deal with factory purchase orders and warehouse inventory, could handle SKU numbers, and manage the freight from China by boat and by air, and he knew how to use QuickBooks—all things I knew little about and truly had no time nor desire to deal with. I knew it wasn't in my arena, and that was okay. It's so important for aspiring business owners to know when to ask for help. To this day, Russell still loves to tell everyone that *he* works for *me*. He gets such a kick out of it.

One of the other major steps I took in the beginning was hiring a company to take over my social media pages. Early on, I didn't know anything about social media or how to use it to boost my business. I got to talking to a friend of mine who had a son my boys' age and a daughter who was a little older. She also had a much younger third child. We'd been friendly for years. We'd go out for drinks or dinner and once on a family ski vacation together.

She told me that her daughter was interning for a new company specializing in social media and marketing and suggested I check it out. So, I did.

The company would charge you a monthly fee to cover their work and ad spend on platforms like Facebook and Instagram. You would, in theory, get assigned an account manager who would plan your monthly social media calendars, create content, and run the ads for your pages.

It sounded good at first, but the more I learned about the business model, the more I knew I'd have to teach myself how to do it all.

The owner of the company was terrific at selling, but he wasn't necessarily good at running a business. He had a bunch of college kids doing the actual work of managing accounts while he was out making sales and taking vacations with his new bride.

But these students were no experts in social media. They might have been studying marketing or communications in college, but that didn't mean they were ready to manage major social media platforms. Far from it. They would plan our monthly social media calendar, with posts for both Facebook and Instagram, and send it to me for approval. The file would have photos or some kind of visual content with captions underneath. Once approved, they'd post those photos on Facebook and Instagram and monitor the engagement. Supposedly, they were running SEO terms and researching the best times to post.

But what ended up happening was that every time they'd send me a calendar to approve, it left me wanting. Content was mostly surf photos or pictures of huge waves. After a while, those photos got boring. And more than that, they didn't speak to our entire audience. Surfers weren't the only ones who bought our boardshorts and beach apparel. Lots of moms were our customers as well. We needed to be marketed as a lifestyle apparel company.

I also had to explain to my account manager that they had to give photo credit when they used other people's images. I didn't think that was something I should have had to do while working with a professional company. The captions for the posts weren't great either. There were a lot of grammar and spelling errors. If I was going through the trouble of approving that calendar, I didn't think I should have to spend so much time editing and rewriting the content.

It started to feel like I should have just done it myself for all the extra time it took. About a year and 10,000 Facebook followers later, I told the owners of the company we needed to go our separate ways. Sure, Just Bones Boardwear had attracted a lot of Facebook followers in that time, but I was doing most of the work! At that point, we'd also started sponsoring some surfers and influencers and expanding our marketing reach.

It took a long time to cut ties with that company. Even though I explained I didn't want to use their services anymore, they wouldn't release control of my admin page on my social media accounts. I had to write to Facebook and explain it was my company, my trademark, and my information. It was an ordeal.

It was beyond gratifying that, after I began posting on my own, we started getting more likes and engagement on posts. The quality of the posts was better, with photos of the surf team and other lifestyle images—not because I became some social media genius but because the posts were authentic and genuine. Our audience liked seeing what was going on with the surfers they were now following, what competitions they were surfing in, and where they were traveling to across the globe. They also adored our influencers who always had the most eye-catching posts. I learned you don't have to be a rocket scientist to get the hang of connecting with your audience on social media.

Since we're a company that has a lot to do with oceans and water, I pay attention to what's going on with water pollution, water waste, and the environment, especially lately. We're facing a global water crisis that's only getting worse. The surfing community doesn't want to see plastic waste or environmental pollution. We've posted about plastic clean up in the ocean and promote charities that focus on providing clean drinking water around the world. Those are both topics that people who like to go to the beach, or who like to go surfing and do other water sports, tend to care about.

Throughout the whole social media fiasco, I realized there is a learning curve to everything. I didn't even know what SEO was when I made my first business account on social media. I didn't know everything I was doing when I first started managing factory production either. If you want to be good at anything, you have to keep at it. You have to pay attention. You have to ask for help when you see someone doing it well or better.

CHAPTER 16

BLURRED LINES

DEALING WITH MANUFACTURING AND MAKING sure we ended up with boardshorts that matched our original tech packs (all the technical information about your product) was no small task. We would count the stitches per inch to make sure they were consistent with our specifications—they have a direct impact on seam strength. You must also verify measurements for all the different components of the garment, including fly opening, waistband height, outseam, inseam, hip, waist, and more. We had to check the functionality of the drawstrings, Velcro, buttons, pocket closures, and quality of the pocket mesh and other trims— not to mention checking all of those details in every single graded size and print you want to go into production. You hire fit models to review and correct the construction of samples and any fit issues—on a real person. Fit models are essentially live mannequins who meet specific measurements required by a designer—bust, waist, thigh, hip, etc. They are not necessarily models you'd see on a fashion show runway.

All these tiny things reviewed in detail were critical before a mass production. You can't tell the factory to go ahead with a production cycle until everything is validated. If you give the green light and later there is a problem, you're still responsible for payment regardless because you gave them approval. And your approval is *always* in writing to the factory.

We had to stay on top of everything to receive quality product, and that meant finding a good factory to meet our needs. At the end of the day, your product is a reflection of your brand. That proved to be tricky after we left our first factory, but we needed to increase our profit margins without an agent middleman. In the beginning, it had been the right decision because many manufacturers work exclusively with distributors and won't even speak to a private company, such as ourselves.

One factory we used had a textile mill printing disaster. It was as if they had never worked with Pantone colors—PMS colors (Pantone Matching System)—or digital printing before, using DTG (direct to garment) printing machines. These machines function in a similar way to an inkjet printer you might have in your home or office but are obviously more complex and require a skilled technician to run them. We had switched from screen-printed fabric after our first factory because it greatly limited our designs since every color requires a separate screen (mesh stencil). Screen printing can be prohibitively costly to set up because each boardshort design that goes into production requires individual screens for *every single* color, and the factory charges you for that. Who wants to start counting colors when creating new collections?! It was dreadful.

Imagine you were making a watercolor painting. You know how the colors bleed together and spread out? Well, that's exactly what our fabric strike offs looked like—Pantones were blended in areas inadvertently, and the result was dull, "muddy" prints. When it's not a watercolor painting, the effect is pretty awful. Part of the issue was ink saturation because it's harder to adjust on fabric than on paper. When fabric absorbs the ink, common problems can occur with saturation and color migration.

Strike offs—which are essentially fabric samples—are necessary to evaluate print scale, and print repeats, to analyze color and saturation, and to check hand feel of the printed fabric. If you have problems with the sample, you can't go ahead with fabric production or your garment will suffer. Any issues must be corrected, and sometimes this entails two or three strike offs to get the printed fabric perfect.

But, of course, production was never that simple.

I sent this factory specific Pantone colors for each subtle color change in our print designs. In case you thought there was just one shade of red, you're wrong. There are multiple shades of red and multiple shades of blue. The variations of a pure color (hue) are tint and shade—how light or dark that color becomes when white and black are added. Tint is when you only add white to a pure color to make it lighter. When you only add black to a pure color, or combination of color, the result is a shade, or darker version, of that color. Then the entire ballgame changes when you *only* add gray to a hue—this is how tone is achieved. It's mind-boggling! It took hours staring at Pantone color guides to find, select, and make note of the exact colors I was looking for.

Even though I gave the factory the precise Pantone colors I wanted them to use for each fabric design, along with the original artwork so they could see the bigger picture, the fabric strike offs came back looking like someone did them blindfolded or drunk. The colors were wrong, there were issues with color saturation, print definition, and many times the scale or repeat of the print was inaccurate. I often had to give them specific details on how to correct the fabric strike offs and send them images with markups, but to little avail.

Maybe they weren't being entirely honest about what equipment they were using or their capabilities. Extended Gamut and Pantone Spot colors make it possible for digital printing to achieve exact colors to match your print designs, but who knew if they even had an experienced printer on hand. Pantone is also used worldwide as the universal language of color between brands and factories because it's a standardized color system with unique numbers for every color. Bearing all this in mind, it never made complete sense to me what the problem was at that textile mill.

Vivian and I finally met with the woman whose family owned this factory when she happened to be in the U.S. for business. I originally met her at a huge industry trade show in Vegas— MAGIC—that's how we started doing business together.

We met up in New Jersey one morning, hoping to have time for small talk before we pounced on her with problems. But before long, we showed her how the fabric strike offs looked when we'd received them for approval. She grabbed the fabric and examined it closely, her face pulling into a frown. She agreed it looked terrible, even before we showed her the original artwork.

Finally, it felt like someone was listening. She could see with her own two eyes why I'd been battling with the factory over fabric printing issues.

"I'm so sorry. We'll make it right," she said.

And she wasted no time. She dialed the number for the manager at the textile mill then and there—mind you, it would have been around midnight in China. I jumped a little as she started emphatically shouting Mandarin into the phone. It felt like something straight out of a movie. Other diners glanced over as she drew attention to our table with all the yelling.

I had no idea what she was saying to the person on the other end of the line, but I could tell she was letting them have it. Vivian, however, spoke fluent Mandarin. It was clear she was trying to stifle a laugh. This went on for about 10 minutes.

The factory owner promised things would improve and that our boardshort fabrics would be impeccable with the next run.

Later, Vivian told me the woman had screamed at the manager, "These fabrics are so ugly, they're making my eyes bleed!"

Well, she wasn't too far from the truth.

Unfortunately, though, the trouble didn't end there.

We received the first round of sample boardshorts from them, which all had metal tips, or aglets, on the drawstrings. We started noticing that those metal tips would often slide right off the drawstrings. To avoid any major dilemma before the problem was fixed, we began to clamp them down tighter with a handheld garment tool before the photo shoot, fashion show, and trade show. It would not bode well for us if a buyer saw this. I was finding little metal aglets all over the office! More importantly, it was a child safety issue! I had emailed the factory, prior to mass production, and made clear that all metal aglets must be reinforced before packaging. We also alerted the company who did our quality control and product inspections at intervals of the production process to keep an eye on it—they ensured our product was meeting our specifications and quality standards before it left China for the States.

That factory proved to be extremely inconsistent. After two years of trying to make it work, and having given them plenty of chances to get their act together, I knew we couldn't continue to do business with them.

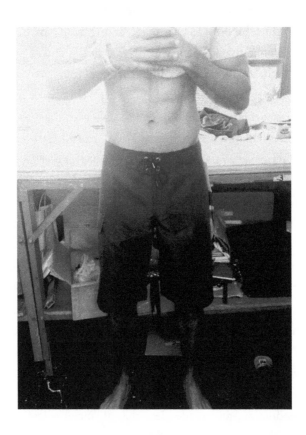

CHAPTER 17

THIS MOTHER OF INVENTION

AMID THE FIGHT TO PROVE I wasn't trying to rip off anyone's trademark and to recover from the accident, I still had to prove my idea was revolutionary and worth patenting.

I wanted desperately to meet the patent examiner face-to-face to show her the prototype. If she could *see* it, I knew she'd understand right away what I had invented. But we had to do the entire interview over a conference call, executed with a speaker in the middle of my lawyer's conference room table.

I sat in the office chair that morning, fighting off nerves and negative thoughts.

Oh my God, this is the worst. I can't even see what this person looks like.

I still wasn't at 100% after the accident, with my memory or even my speech. At times, I would find myself forgetting words and getting tripped up trying to explain things. I worried I'd screw up the presentation.

I wrote out some bullet points just in case, but for the most part, I vowed to stick to my script. I'd described the boardshort's hidden adjustable waist a thousand times—why should this be any different?

I took a deep breath as the phone rang. I was as ready as I'd ever be.

The patent examiner asked me to tell the story behind the boardshort and how I came up with my idea to make them fully adjustable, while still appearing like a fixed-waist boardshort, and the technology I used. She wanted to make sure it was an authentic idea—that I hadn't taken from somewhere else. She let me talk a lot and asked me some questions, but I had no trouble launching straight into my marketing pitch.

I had the presentation down pat, and I truly think that was my saving grace. I could give that speech in my sleep. I explained the product like I would to a retail buyer interested in some functional boardshorts.

When the call ended, I felt a moment of panic. Did I give her enough detail? Did I explain everything I needed to? Surely, I'd left something significant and persuasive out.

"How do you think it went?" I asked my lawyer.

"I thought it went remarkably well!" she said. "And now we wait."

There wasn't much else to do at that point. My lawyer had faith we'd get the patent.

Today, there is a wide variety of swimwear options to flatter many body types. One of the biggest trends in the last few years is "Daddy and me" matching swimwear. Many swim companies are capitalizing on this trend and make the same prints for their men's and boys' swimwear so fathers and sons can match on vacation or during their beach outings. It's so cute, the "mini-me" look. Some men pick out matching boardshorts or women buy the matching prints as gifts.

Just Bones Boardwear began matching family prints organically several years ago. Men would come into our trade show booth and tell us they thought our boardshorts were awesome—then they'd ask why they didn't come in men's sizes too. Many buyers remarked that they would love to order matching prints for toddlers, boys, and men, so it seemed like a natural evolution to us. Our retailers began giving us the same feedback—that men wanted the same boys' boardshort prints for themselves. And when they discovered the hidden adjustable waist, that was the icing on the cake!

That's when we sincerely started considering entering the men's swimwear market. Today, our men's boardshorts account for 50% of our sales! They are extremely popular at resort destinations and menswear shops. If you had asked me when I started my business with only boys' boardshorts if I thought that would ever happened, I would probably have said no. So, we have been pleasantly surprised.

On a personal note, I'm a bikini girl—much to my husband's pleasure and my sons' dismay. I was born and raised in Miami where it was the norm to show a lot of skin. I can't remember *anyone* wearing a one-piece suit when I was a teenager. Now, however, I keep one tucked away in a drawer *just in case* I need something slightly more conservative.

I have a passion for designing bikinis too, even if Just Bones Boardwear is predominantly about boardshorts. Recently I designed a bikini—called the Eve Wrap—that uses a retro-style interlocking buckle closure on both sides of the bottom. I love that feature, as it reminds me of the stretch rainbow belts we used to wear as kids—I find my inspiration everywhere. It has a wrap bikini top and is made out of an ombré floral fabric. It's hard for me to pick favorites because all my designs feel like my babies, but that bikini might just be it.

CHAPTER 18

BIRTHDAY SUITS AND BOTTLE CLUBS

NDIA HICKS MAY HAVE BEEN my first major client, but she wasn't the only famous person I bumped into over the years. Some of the Miami Heat players and other celebrities hung out at a club where we went for afterparties a few times during Miami Swim Week. Once, when I had been graciously seated at a prime VIP table with some friends, a random guy sat on the arm of the couch in our section. He was in the VIP area right next to ours.

I said hello—because what else are you supposed to do?

An uptight guy hovering in the background nearly jumped down my throat for it.

"Hey! Leave him alone. He's the point guard for the Houston Rockets."

Well, good grief, how was I supposed to know that? Maybe the fact that the guy was still taller than me, sitting down, even as I stood wearing heels should have tipped me off that he was a basketball player.

I said to him very quietly, "I have to tell my son who I met. He loves basketball."

It turns out it was James Harden. About a month later, he was being interviewed on television, and I pointed out to Russell that he was the basketball player I had bumped into. Both he and Josh freaked out and could not believe I had been in the presence of a basketball superstar and MVP *and* that I hadn't known whom I was speaking to.

It seemed as if there was always someone famous or interesting at these late-night events. It was fun in the beginning to appear in Getty Images while hanging out around models and celebrities who attended these exclusive soirées, but staying out until all hours takes its toll when you have to be up at 5:30 a.m. the next morning. Eventually, you come to realize you're surrounded by all these beautiful people and teenyboppers who do not have corporate jobs. And the parties don't even kick off until 11 p.m. To what end?

It's impossible to party like that continually and still wake up for work early in the morning. I decided I needed sleep more than I needed the entertainment these parties could provide. Besides, they caused more stress and drama than they were worth.

As we grew and got into a good rhythm, some of the extravagance lost its luster. I quickly learned that runway shows were breeding grounds for drama.

The producer and manager of the fashion show platform I'd committed to, let's call him Bryan, once asked me to help get him into a trendy Miami nightclub. He wanted VIP access, especially after he heard a famous DJ was booked to play that night.

"You grew up in Miami," he said. "Can you help us get in?"

I had made the mistake of carelessly mentioning to Bryan's assistant—let's call her Cassie—that one of Russell's friends was a partner at this hot Miami club. He and Russell grew up together and kept in touch over the years, even as Russell went on to law school and his friend went on to manage fighters, and later become a real estate mogul.

"Do you think you can hook us up at the club?" she asked. "We really want to check it out. I heard it's seriously hard to get in."

It *was* going to be exceptionally hard to land a table during Swim Week, especially because celebrities like Brody Jenner were lined up to DJ. I knew the epic nightclub would be packed every night, with lines to enter curling around the corner at all hours.

"I can ask, but I don't really know that I can promise," I told her.

I asked Russell if he could contact his friend to help me out. His friend had hooked us up a couple times in the past, but I don't like asking people for favors like that. Russell made the call, but his friend didn't answer right away. That wasn't unusual. This guy traveled a lot on private jets back and forth from Miami to Los Angeles. And why shouldn't he? The guy was a self-made millionaire. He didn't have to be on call for friends looking to leverage his connections.

Finally, Russell called me back with good news. It was the 11th hour, but his friend had secured us a VIP table upstairs for eight people, which was incredible considering it was last minute.

I tracked Cassie down to tell her the good news.

"I got us a table for eight tonight," I said.

"Oh, don't worry about it; we have a table already," she replied.

In the midst of me pulling strings I didn't want to pull, I guess she "forgot" to tell me one of the models they worked with had reserved a VIP table for them all, thanks to her uber-wealthy boyfriend. They paid close to $10,000 just to sit there that night. When you get a VIP table at any of these hot nightclubs in South Beach, you have a "minimum spend"—a certain amount of money you must spend on alcohol of your choice. Even if you don't drink that much, you still get charged—so you might as well drink it!

I still had a VIP table for eight. I couldn't simply back out now, not when Russell's friend had gone through the trouble to reserve it for me. Anyone else would have paid at least $8,000 "minimum spend" for it. And our table had an eagle-eye view of the entire club, including of the DJ booth!

So, I figured I'd invite some of my employees and whoever else happened to be around. It would be a bonus for them during a week filled with 10-hour work days. I invited one of the models I had booked a few times and knew was in Miami for Swim Week. Among the employees who came was Todd. He brought a friend of his along, whose parents had a vacation place in Miami Beach. I included a couple of my good friends from Miami too.

We arrived at the club around the same time as Bryan and his posse. I saw him and his crew get out of a limo and walk up to the VIP line. They didn't even notice us standing by the club entrance and, worse, pretended they didn't see one of the other fashion show designers waiting in line whom we *all* knew. They walked right past him without even saying hello. I'm guessing they didn't want him or his boyfriend to be on their tab. He'd done a lot to help Bryan out with his fashion show sponsors, and for what?

The fashion industry can be wicked and two-faced. People like Bryan will be nice to you when they *want* something but then walk right past you like they don't know your name when you don't have anything to offer them. Their attitude is, "What did you do for me lately, hon?" Sadly, they will end up all alone and with no genuine friends.

Because I knew one of the owners, we didn't have to wait in the club line. As we walked in, I tapped the other designer on the shoulder.

"Do you guys want to come in with me? You can sit at our table, if you want to."

"Oh my God, you are so sweet," he said.

He and his boyfriend sat with us for a while, but bought their own drinks at the bar because he didn't want to mooch off me. That wasn't his style. Eventually, they left the table to explore and see more of the club.

It was a strange mix of people, but I thought it would be nice to show them all a good time. It wasn't every day we could all just walk into one of the hottest clubs in Miami and have a first-class table to boot.

At these clubs all the alcohol is marked up insanely high. At some of them, you might spend $400 for a bottle of Grey Goose, which you can easily get for $30 at a liquor store. A bottle of Patrón is equally ridiculous.

Even so, I ordered a nice bottle of champagne for the table. This was in addition to the vodka and tequila with mixers I had already gotten for everyone. I figured that I should spend some money on booze and service because someone else could have sat at our premium table.

And despite our motley crew, we all had a great time that night.

Bryan and Cassie's table was right below us on the main level of the club. There were probably 15 people sitting there, squished into the circular booth and sitting on the flat backside of it against the wall. They were all getting wasted.

Typically, security stops people from going past the ropes to get to the VIP tables on the upper level of the club, but somehow Bryan managed to come upstairs and find me.

"Oh, Jen, how are you?" he said.

He'd clearly already had several drinks, as per usual.

"Let's go say hi to Brody Jenner," he said. "You know the club owners, right? I want a picture with Brody."

Surprisingly, he convinced me to go downstairs and get closer to the DJ booth, but I told Bryan I wasn't going to talk to the bouncers or tell them I knew anyone who worked at the club. I thought he'd let it go, but he didn't.

"I'm not going to stand here like a groupie trying to talk these bouncers into letting you speak to the DJ," I said. "Besides, Brody and his buddies are spinning right now and swigging tequila straight from a bottle of 1942."

I eventually walked away and went back to my table, annoyed with myself for letting him talk me into going anywhere with him in the first place. I hated walking through throngs of people because it made me feel claustrophobic. And the club was beyond packed that night.

By the time we left the club, it was nearly 3 a.m. People were still lined up around the block to get in. I later learned from Todd, who decided it was more fun to hang out at the downstairs booth overflowing with champagne to meet their minimum spend, that Bryan regularly had a staff member assigned to getting him home safe because he got so drunk.

Inevitably, Bryan then asked me for help with an afterparty for the next Swim Week. My childhood friend's mother was in real estate, and her real estate partner's son was the owner of the hottest nightclub in South Beach. It was the hub for celebrities, entertainers, wannabes, and professional athletes. My connection was flimsy at best, but Bryan was convinced I could make it happen. "Please, Jen, will you help me out here?" He always laid it on thick like you were best friends forever.

Reluctantly, I agreed. Still, I didn't like being put in the position of asking anyone for favors—especially when it wasn't even my event! How on earth had I become the personal party planner for Bryan?

Looking back, I realize I hadn't yet fully grasped his mean streak. He was good at making you feel like he was your best buddy, like he was helping you, until he didn't see a need for you anymore. However, he had a way of sucking people in. So, I tried to help.

I cold-called the club and politely asked to speak with the owner by name. This brought back memories of my days working in the conference business before I got pregnant. I got passed around to a couple people before eventually being able to speak with their marketing guy. He asked me to follow up with a detailed email explaining what we were hoping for at Bryan's afterparty, in exchange for what Bryan's platform could provide them. After multiple email exchanges, details being fleshed out about VIP wristbands, models, logos, booze, VIP nightclub tables, and cross-marketing efforts, the club agreed to host an afterparty during Swim Week *and* to advertise it. This was huge! I'd always been good at this kind of thing because I used to make these deals for a living, but I hadn't done it in years—it was good to know I still had it in me! I had a real sense of satisfaction from closing the deal, even though it wasn't for Just Bones Boardwear. Naturally, we would still benefit from being able to showcase our bikinis during the club afterparty.

I had spent close to an hour writing the meticulous email laying out every detail regarding what Bryan's platform could provide to the club in exchange for the venue and afterparty. I tried to make it sound as if the club was getting something undeniably good in exchange for the party, but in reality, they were still the ones doing us a huge favor. It was currently the most prestigious and glamorous South Beach nightclub, continually star-studded, and where *everyone* wanted to be seen.

After all, for an average night it can cost anywhere from $60 to $100 merely to step foot inside the club, depending on the DJ and weeknight, let alone to buy drinks. The price tag goes up for weekend nights and special events. The most elite and well-known photographers were there every night taking photos. There were scantily clad dancers staged around the nightclub. It felt like you were in Vegas. All those things would add to the prestige of the afterparty and had the potential to offer major exposure for the designers who showcased their swimwear.

The managers replied, asking for a conference call, so naturally I agreed to it.

I soon found myself on the phone pitching Bryan's business. It was not even to benefit my own brand! I told them what Bryan promised to provide the club, including premier front row runway seats, and asked what they were proposing for an afterparty. What they offered genuinely surprised me. We received a blowout list of lavish party perks and contributions from the club and much more than we anticipated.

Bryan offered to list the nightclub as a fashion show sponsor, include their logo on the fashion show invitations, and promote them across all his digital marketing platforms. The club provided 500 free VIP wristbands for guests. They agreed to let the fashion designers use the catwalk in front of their DJ station, so our models (the stipulation being female only) could do a mini fashion show wearing our swimwear, and to let their dancers wear the designers' swimwear on stage. Surprisingly, the club also granted us five VIP tables, complete with gratuitous champagne and booze for *the entire night* and contributed an hour of complimentary cocktails at the bar for guests entering the club wearing a VIP wristband. Normally, when you reserve a VIP table at these trendy nightclubs, they can cost anywhere from $2,500–$12,000 and upward for the night.

I scored all this for Bryan's party for *free*.

In exchange, Bryan said I could be the first designer of the night on the runway. I couldn't help but roll my eyes. It hardly seemed to make up for all the work and time I'd put in to secure this incredible afterparty. But hey, he did say I could choose a couple extra models for my show.

Bryan and I were supposed to meet with the club managers the day before the party. We scheduled a meeting with them in the morning, before the model casting call for the fashion shows. The club's corporate offices were right down the street from where the casting call was being held.

I got dressed and was there ahead of time. I sent my assistant and a summer intern to set up for the model casting so everything would be ready when I arrived after the meeting.

Then I waited. And waited. And waited. But Bryan didn't show or call.

The managers and I sat in awkward silence for a short while. I could feel them staring at me. Eventually, I excused myself to the restroom so I could call Bryan behind closed doors.

"Bryan, where are you? We're both supposed to be at this meeting with the club managers to finalize tomorrow's afterparty details."

"Oh, hon, I'm waiting for some things to be delivered. I can't be there," he replied.

"Bryan, you're supposed to be here," I said sharply. "They're expecting to meet with you in person."

"Jen, you can handle it. I believe in you," he said. Then he hung up.

I have never been so mortified. I was ashamed. These guys were organizing and *giving* us this phenomenal party, and Bryan was being a prima donna who couldn't even show up for a meeting he'd agreed to. He had many people, and multiple assistants, who worked for him. Someone else could have easily received his delivery.

Trying to will my face not to turn red with embarrassment, I walked back into the room to confront the club managers. Fake it until you make it, I told myself. I put on a smile.

"Bryan had an emergency," I said, "but he can join us via speakerphone on my cell."

I couldn't believe he'd embarrassed me like that after I put so much work into securing that party for him. I could tell that the managers weren't happy with the situation either. But thankfully, I smoothed it all over when I got Bryan on my cell for what turned out to be a short and simple call about the upcoming event. I thanked the managers for their time, everything they were doing for the afterparty, and then promised to send them some of our boardshorts after my return back home. We exchanged VIP wristbands for both the club party and the fashion show seats. After being so humiliated, I felt a small sense of victory that I had complete control now with all the VIP club wristbands in my possession!

The night of the party, things started to unravel....

I'd asked a few of the models walking for my runway show to work at the afterparty. After all, it was only going to take a half hour or so to model the swimwear, plus they were getting some nice VIP perks. They had confirmed during the model casting that they would participate. It wasn't a paid gig, but I explained there were many opportunities for terrific publicity and media coverage at this club. Nevertheless, since it was Bryan's fashion show platform and theoretically *his* afterparty, his employees were the ones in charge of booking the models and confirming their obligation for the night.

But, as the timing for the DJ catwalk grew closer, the models were nowhere to be found. And Bryan was drunk.

After scouring the entire crowded club, I realized the models were all together in a smaller, secluded VIP section roped off and guarded by a huge bouncer. No matter what I told the bouncer about my connection to the party and the club managers, he refused to let me in. So, I had to resort to running around in heels to look for one of the managers.

"Rob!" I shouted over the loud music when I finally found him. "We need to get the models out of your VIP section in the back of the club. Will you *please* tell the bouncer to let us in?"

But it turned out the models didn't want the gig anymore, and they didn't want to leave the VIP section they had gotten very comfortable in. They said there wasn't enough of an incentive to do the "extra fashion show" for *free*; therefore, they didn't feel like doing it. They were having more fun drinking and dancing.

I was livid. This was something Bryan's booking manager was supposed to have handled. Of course, he hadn't bothered to figure out those details.

Thankfully, *one* of the models who regularly walked for Bryan's shows did follow through. She was a bona fide professional who'd worked runway shows many times before and during many fashion weeks worldwide. She wasn't just a model for Swim Week, she was a seasoned veteran. She was there with her rich boyfriend at their own private VIP table—away from the party—and she knew the name of the game. She instantly got up and headed to the back room to get her hair and makeup done.

In desperation, one of Bryan's employees grabbed an attractive woman in the audience and asked if she wanted to model for us. She agreed to it, though she refused to change her unflattering shoes. I honestly believe she only agreed to model because she had been drinking, and, after all, doesn't everyone want their 15 minutes of fame? I was not happy. We were not even close to the 10 models we had promised the club. The "bikini" fashion show was advertised as part of the club entertainment that night, and we were about to blow it. Bryan was about to ruin everything.

Since we were short on models, we convinced one of the other designers to wear her own swimwear and join the other two models on the catwalk. She was sort of a southern debutante, who had aged a little, and who had probably been in pageants growing up. She was more than willing to be in the limelight again.

Soon enough, the designers were arguing about whose swimwear would go on stage first—even though Bryan had given the club a list ahead of time for the brand logos to be illuminated in order across the enormous LED screens mounted everywhere. I promptly decided to take charge. After all, I had organized the entire shebang!

"I'm going first," I said. "Put my logo up there on the screens." Bryan was supposed to go first, but he was so sloshed he didn't even notice. If he did, he didn't comment, and neither did Cassie. They knew this whole thing was falling apart at the seams—there were no models and no real fashion show.

The two models (one a pinch hitter) went out wearing my swimsuits and did a great job—it just wasn't the 10 bikini models we'd promised. I set the party up, so naturally I was the one who looked like the jackass and would be blamed. I was silently praying nobody important noticed how short we were on bikini models.

But lucky for me, the models were out on the catwalk in my swimwear while the live entertainment was performing! She was singing right at the center of the two models. And the club dancers were also rocking my bikinis! All of this was caught on camera by World Red Eye photographers! The moment would be preserved forever.

In an effort to salvage the night, I told Bryan how terrific the runway shows were and how fortunate we all were to be part of such a sensational afterparty. I even gave the woman from the audience $100 for modeling. Not one other designer stepped up to pitch in monetarily, even though they all witnessed me handing over the cash. At Bryan's request, I had already left two dozen Just Bones Boardwear silver logo swag bags at the club entrance for VIP guests. This was all at our own cost. That was the last year I worked with Bryan for a runway show.

Unfortunately, there are many Bryans in the industry—people who want you to bear the brunt of the burden without offering you much of value in return.

Thanks to interactions like these, I realized how important it was to have a thick skin. I'm not sure I could have handled it all if I hadn't developed that protective armor living in New York. To deal with people like Bryan, you have to remember their behavior isn't a reflection of who you are or how you're performing. You can't take everything to heart or take everything personally. You have to let it roll off you otherwise you'll be a basket case.

Some events with industry people make me laugh as I look back on them.

For our first "real" destination location photo shoot, I boarded a plane and flew to Exuma in the Bahamas with my stylist, a photographer, and two models. We were just launching the bikini line so Russell let me splurge a little on this shoot.

On each day of the shoot, we had to take a tiny, rented motorboat out to various areas the photographer had scouted where the tides were low. The first day, we motored to a remote sandbar where we spent hours getting shots of every new bikini sample. As the hours passed, the tide went out farther and the teeny sandbar we were on transformed into our very own temporary private island. Despite its beauty, the sun was hot, and the hours were long as my stylist and I ran around trying to keep our model happy. She would take the bikinis off and fling them into the wet sand rather than hand them over like anyone living in civilized society. My stylist, and friend, had to work overtime to keep the model fresh and photo ready, regardless of her continued complaints about her fake lashes. Believe it or not, we both had to rub suntan lotion on her body *for* her!

When every bikini had been photographed and it was time to go, we had to sit and wait another 45 minutes while the model ran around the beach buck naked and the photographer did a freelance sunset shoot. What was going on? I most definitely did not pay for this! I was hot, hungry, tired, and wanted a shower. My stylist declared that she could not stop thinking about the movie *Blue Lagoon* after watching this interesting development.

At that point, she and I exchanged knowing glances—the model and photographer were definitely sleeping together, and they didn't care one bit that we were tired, sweaty, and hangry.

To make things more complicated, we were staying in such a remote area at an online rental property that we had to buy all our groceries in advance at a small island market and cook everything ourselves. That wouldn't have been a problem except the only people who knew how to cook were me and the photographer. I had certainly not paid good money nor traveled there to be a cook every night!

And, of course, the model demanded fish and salad. No rice, no pasta, no wine for her. Her body was a temple. Being from LA, the photographer was totally on board with that diet as well.

When the stylist and I finally broke out the wine and the chocolate—truly our saving grace—they looked at us like we had three heads.

Some incidents with people in the fashion industry bordered on creepy. Once, I worked with a male model who legitimately came on to me. He said something about how he would sleep with his clients all the time. It was as if he expected me to want or even require it, like he was just a piece of meat. I simply told him "Hey, that's not my scene."

It's kind of sad. It's not only the male models, but the women in the industry too. I think they're so accustomed to dealing with objectification, they are not used to being treated like regular people beyond their physical appearance.

I was no stranger to sexual harassment, though most of my experience was outside of the swimwear business. At my very first job after college, my boss called me at home late one night. He was drunk and hitting on me, and he asked to come over. No one really did anything about it, even after I reported the incident to HR. Their idea of "handling it" was moving me to another department in the company. A marketing guy was disturbingly inappropriate with me the following year at the annual company Christmas party. But that was the 1990s—there were never any consequences for behavior like that back then.

The harassment was the worst when I worked as a cocktail waitress at a hotel bar when I was 19 and still in college. Some older businessmen would put their hotel room keys on the table next to their tip as a subtle invitation for me to come upstairs to their rooms. They weren't even embarrassed to do it.

Thankfully, not everyone in the industry is terrible. I worked with other fashion show platforms and producers who knew how to be professional. They also wanted to help designers and had no expectations of favors in return. One producer promised a video shoot of me and my newest collection during our beach photo shoot right before Swim Week and actually followed through. Afterward, they filmed an interview with me on the beach, then put it on a cable television show that aired worldwide.

The very same producer also got me invited to be interviewed along with her for NBC News. They were doing a segment on Swim Week and filming on location where our runway show would later be held. I scrambled to buy a new dress and prepare for the TV interview, all while getting ready for a runway show and Swim Week. The NBC reporter asked me about being a designer in the same breath and sentence as mentioning Roberto Cavalli! The interview didn't last very long, but it was so exciting! I could not wait to see the news story!

It was refreshing to work with someone who went out of their way to support me rather than take advantage of me.

The charity events I participated in were just as inspiring. It felt good to be surrounded by other companies, and some celebrities, who were willing to come together and give back to the community. The work I did with those organizations aimed at expanding access to the arts for underprivileged children, raising money for children with special needs, or sponsoring local surf events. One summer, we sponsored and showcased our swimwear at a Hamptons White Party! Boy, were our silver logo swag bags popular at that White Party. Robin McGraw, Dr. Phil's wife, recognized for her work in philanthropy, was there promoting her new book. So many movers and shakers were willing to go out of their way to be exceedingly nice—whether it was to the kids they were serving or the companies that signed up to help or sponsor.

I forgot what it was like to be around people who didn't walk all over others to get what they wanted. More than that, it was motivating to know there were highly successful famous people out there who didn't use their brands or fame to boost their personal image.

CHAPTER 19

NO ROOM AT THE INN!

I TREAT EVERYONE, FROM MY BUSINESS employees to my housekeepers, with generosity. Some of the stay-at-home moms used to criticize me for it. They'd ask why we'd take our housekeeper out for her birthday every year. That never made sense to me. If someone worked for you and took good care of your children every day for 12 years, why *wouldn't* you treat them well in return?

Still today, I hear from former housekeepers and babysitters, even though we moved to Arizona. We stay connected over text message or on social media, and I'm happy for that.

I firmly believe that the way you treat people matters. That applies to people who don't work for you too.

I'd go out of my way to talk to the hotel bellmen and be nice whenever I traveled. I'd give them extra Surf Expo swag whenever I had it after the show. They all knew me by name and always said hello when they saw me at the hotel. The same was true when our family vacationed. The bellmen would even remember Josh and Jake by name. A couple years ago, while in Orlando for a show, I got extremely sick and had to go to urgent care for antibiotics. I stayed in the hotel room for an extra day or two while I recovered. When I finally emerged, the hotel staff were genuinely concerned about my well-being. "How are you? We haven't seen you in over twenty-four hours!" they said. It was so nice to feel like I had extended family on these long, often stressful, business trips.

One year, our booking for every hotel room got screwed up, and there were no rooms available at all when I went to check in. A front desk employee tried to send us to a dingy hotel many blocks away from the convention center.

Greg, one of the bellmen, called the front desk manager and convinced him to take care of us as loyal, repeat guests, who stayed there twice a year when our biannual trade show was at the convention center. The manager wound up placing us in one of their two enormous presidential suites. That happened solely because all the bellmen went to bat for me. Not all the hotel guests without rooms that night were as fortunate. Many had to relocate to other hotels—some very inconvenient to the show.

One of our interns was a quiet, diligent, and professional young woman. She worked hard throughout the summer. When her internship ended, she shared with me during her exit interview how much she had learned from the job.

"I was so introverted and shy, it was hard for me to make cold calls to people," she said. "Now, I'm so happy I did it. I know that when I have to start making calls for phone interviews to get jobs after college, I'll feel more confident. I'm happy I worked here and learned that skill, amongst others."

It made me feel good that she got something out of the internship and wasn't just biding her time that summer for college credit.

CHAPTER 20

COMMUTER CATASTROPHES

E VEN THOUGH I WAS HEALING physically and mentally from the accident, I couldn't escape the hazardous traffic. Two of my employees left after horrible events on the roads in town.

One of my interns had eventually begun working as a full-time employee doing marketing work. She was especially good at helping us set up different accounts we needed, like Snapchat. I let her take on more responsibility as time went on. Plus, she was a pro at showing the ropes to new interns and working special events.

She was scheduled to work with me at the next trade show in Huntington Beach, California. I left two days early to visit a friend in Calabasas before setup day for the show.

But when she left work one night, she got into a frightening accident as she was leaving Millburn on Old Short Hills Road. Another vehicle rear-ended her, slamming her into the car ahead and totaling her car. An ambulance had to come for her. She lost consciousness at some point when her head hit the steering wheel and got a terrible concussion. Before going to the hospital, she managed to text Russell because she was supposed to leave for California the next day.

Our accidents weren't the same, but I understood why, a month later, she said she couldn't work for us anymore. I had initially assumed she needed some time off to heal and to figure out her transportation situation. But that accident changed her.

She told us then it was because she couldn't yet afford to get a new car, but I could tell a large part of it was because she didn't want to have to drive into Millburn. In addition, I found out she was having trouble just being in a car again.

I get it.

I lost her over that accident.

And she wasn't the only one.

Our office was right across the street from the train station on Essex Street. It had an overpass and a parking garage. Commuters were often sprinting across the street to catch the train or to rush home at the end of the working day, and drivers were often speeding to make the light.

Another one of my employees was leaving work one night when she witnessed the aftermath of a dreadful pedestrian accident. She turned right by the commuter garage to head home, and suddenly, traffic had stopped. There had been an accident straight ahead of her. Car versus pedestrian.

As she slowly pulled forward, she saw a woman lying in the middle of the road. The accident had just occurred, and in that moment, she couldn't tell if the woman was still alive. She had to pull over, she was crying so hard. She sat there in her car while the ambulance came, and she watched first responders take the woman away. Distraught, she then called her mother to tell her what had happened.

It seriously impacted her.

She talked about the accident a lot. Soon, she started pulling away, making excuses for why she wanted to work from home. Eventually, it got to the point where we couldn't work with her anymore because we truly needed her at the office.

These accidents impact people psychologically. They create tension, mental anxiety, and emotional trauma far beyond the people who were immediately involved in them. Not only had a car accident upended my life when I got hit but also now other car accidents were scaring away my best employees. They were terrified.

———————

According to *The Item*, between 2003 and 2015, 12 pedestrians—*including me*—were hit by cars at the intersection of Essex and Main Street. During that same time frame, 26 pedestrians were hit by cars at the intersections of Millburn and Main Street.[14]

In March 2015, an Essex County spokesperson told *The Item* they saw no reason to make any additional changes to the intersections.[15] When I heard that, I just couldn't believe it! No reason to make any changes? How could they not see that there was a problem? I personally knew two other women who were hit in one of those intersections. One of them, a mom like me, was in a coma for three months. She had to have multiple surgeries. She could have died. Thankfully, she made it through, but she looks different now. The fractures to her face and the surgery she needed made her almost unrecognizable the first time I saw her again.

My life changed so much after the accident. It took a lot of work to heal. It was hard on my family. It almost derailed my business. I could only imagine the impact and the ripple effects all those other accidents had on all those other people.

And the accidents kept coming.

Once, a friend of ours asked me, out of the blue, to come speak at a town meeting about my accident. His son played varsity lacrosse with Josh.

"I'm going to be speaking about why they need to change the traffic patterns," he said. "Do you think you'd be willing to tell your story? I believe it would have a major impact if you came and spoke."

I didn't know what to say. I was so caught off guard. At this point in my life, I was in no condition to speak openly about the accident. I was still working through PTSD and a lawsuit. Inside my head, I was screaming, *No effing way! It's not gonna happen!*

"I understand if you don't want to," he said, "but I think it would make a huge difference."

I told him I couldn't because I was still in the middle of litigation. And genuinely, I imagine my lawyer would have advised me against it.

Honestly, I knew it would benefit him and everyone else if I did speak at the meeting, but I couldn't bring myself to do it. He just didn't understand what that would be like for me. I was simply not ready to talk about my trauma.

I don't think people realize the tremendous emotional impact talking about trauma can have on a person. At that point, merely sitting and talking about the accident brought it all back. I was unable to control the emotion that came flooding in like a riptide taking hold of my body. In that instant, when someone says something that triggers PTSD, you can't control your reaction. It's a purely raw thing that just happens.

Thankfully, things started to change, even without me reliving one of the worst days of my life in front of a huge crowd of people.

In December 2014, the town finally considered some serious work to address the dangerous traffic problem,[16] especially after the number of pedestrians being hit by cars at the town's dangerous intersections kept growing.

The city ultimately began to review implementing the Complete Streets program,[17] a product of Smart Growth America, a nonprofit based in Washington, D.C., that aims to foster safer, equitable urban development policies.[18]

According to the program, at least 54,435 pedestrians were hit and killed by drivers between 2010 and 2019.[19]

The Complete Streets program aims to reduce the number of pedestrian deaths on roadways by integrating safer planning, design, construction, operation, and maintenance and transportation networks.[20]

In Millburn, the initiative called for extensive changes, including a prohibition on left turns in some places, in particular where I got hit, and reducing Millburn Avenue from three lanes to two lanes, from the center of the downtown area to the Essex Street and Millburn Avenue intersection.[21] It called for sidewalks to be widened with bump-outs at the intersection. It also called for the pedestrian island with its two crosswalks in the area to be removed in favor of a new traffic light.[22]

The goal was to slow traffic down and create more buffers between people and cars. Some people worried about how those changes would impact traffic in other parts of the town. Others, especially downtown business owners, were angry with the idea of more construction. Commuters were grumpy at the idea of having to drive through the town more slowly.[23]

But, well, that was the whole point. The Complete Streets initiative would slow traffic going through downtown. It would also discourage commuters from using it to cut through to the highway or the train station.

As the town continued to review the plan, I couldn't escape the conversation no matter how hard I tried. I'd been personally impacted. The accident changed the course of my life. Yet, for some reason, people around town thought I might be interested in hearing about how much of an inconvenience the construction works would be.

If people had to take five minutes longer to figure out where to park because the town was safer for anyone on foot, so be it! No matter how much people felt put out, nobody else would get hit the same way I had been. With the proposed changes, drivers could no longer make that left turn.

CHAPTER 21

LITTLE HOUSE OF HR HORRORS

WE WENT OUT OF OUR way to treat our employees well—that's why it was so upsetting to me when employees betrayed us or lied to us. You'd think it would be harder to do what they did, but some of it, I think, is just human nature—everyone is dealing with their own issues in life. Everyone has bad days. But let me tell you—regardless of that, we did have some awful employees.

A young man, we'll call him Michael, was one of the first people I hired outside of the moms. He did a great job for us. One of the biggest pitfalls for him wasn't truly his fault—he was just young and fresh out of college. He still had a lot to learn.

He was a quiet guy, but he'd worked with surf apparel before, and he was personable. He needed a little bit of a push at the trade shows to interact with buyers, but that's true of many of the younger employees.

Michael stayed with us for a couple years and was productive at work. He was able to open some new accounts and was valuable at trade shows, especially because he surfed and could speak effortlessly to surf shop owners. We had no issues with him—until he slept with Erika.

When I hired Erika, she acted as if she was doing us a favor. She had a job with a designer clothing brand before she came to us, though I later learned that her entire accessories department had been eliminated.

I suppose she was biding her time until her affluent boyfriend proposed and she felt like she could quit. They often went to his parents' country house on the weekends. At some point, she mentioned his family was quite wealthy. She was *obsessed* with getting married. In the meantime, she had a job. However, she wasn't a good worker, and she hardly ever made an effort. She fooled around all the time and managed to barely do anything while pretending to be busy.

Erika and Michael both came to Swim Week that July. As usual, I took our employees out for dinner and drinks and an afterparty.

They both had a decent amount to drink and seemed to get a little closer and more flirtatious as the night went on, but I thought nothing of it at the time.

Later, I learned Michael didn't go back to his own room that night. Jake, my son, was also helping us out with the trade show during Swim Week. It was last minute, so he was sharing a hotel room with Michael. He was too young to take out to the parties, but while we were all hanging out at the pool, he had overheard Erika mention that her boyfriend didn't care if she had casual hookups as long as it didn't mean anything. How come *I* never heard any of this employee gossip?

I hoped it would only be awkward for a little while, but it was insufferable.

The two of them started acting strange soon after we returned to New Jersey. If one of them was in the office, the other would find some excuse not to come in to work that day. For Erika, it was a fling that didn't mean anything. She had her boyfriend, the country home, and their future all mapped out. But it clearly meant something to Michael, and he couldn't let it go. Soon, he announced that he was moving to California. Although he didn't say so explicitly, we all knew he simply wanted to get away from the situation after Miami.

What honestly got to me most was that we lost a good employee because of a bad one. Erika wasn't doing any work, she was a huge pain in my ass, and then she had to go sleep with a guy while she had a boyfriend.

I wanted to shake her and yell, *Shame on you!*

Eventually, after numerous missed workdays, and catching her in a blatant lie, we let Erika go. It was actually a relief.

Then there was Todd, the worst of the worst.

Todd came to me as an intern. He was recommended by a friend who knew him when they worked together at a previous job, so I decided to interview him for a summer position. I liked that he was interested in fashion and that he was a student at FIT. Additionally, he'd previously worked for Victoria's Secret as an intern and had experience working backstage at their fashion shows. What a bonus!

Initially, Todd was a very hard worker. There was no task too menial for him. That was perfect for me because, back then, there was a lot of menial work to be done. If needed, he'd even come over on a Saturday and help me work through selecting exact Pantone colors for multiple prints before we could give our factory the artwork to move forward with fabric strike offs. The painstaking process of matching Pantones worked best in natural light, and sometimes that meant working weekends. We had tight deadlines, and luckily, Todd understood when they had to be met. We spent hours making sure the factory would use the precise colors we wanted and provided them with a list of our Pantone color numbers (unique color codes) for each boardshort and bikini print.

Todd never complained, even when the hours stretched on. He was dedicated then and did whatever it took to get the job done.

When he graduated college, I hired him as a full-time employee. He started working more consistent hours when we leased a larger office space and had room for more people to come in and work on site.

The problems began when he got a new boyfriend. It seemed that his boyfriend was a terrible influence on him. When Todd still lived at home, he came across as a nice young man, despite complaining endlessly about sharing a room with his brother. But as soon as he moved in with his boyfriend, he started calling in sick when he wasn't sick. He started cutting corners, and his work suffered.

Then, late one Friday, we had a fitting scheduled for the new bikini samples.

When I first launched the Bikini Party line, I preferred to use one particular yoga fitness model for the bikini fittings. She was in great shape, and our bikini separates fit her measurements well.

I woke up with terrible bronchitis and a raging fever that Friday, so I planned to stay home and out of the way. I knew Todd could handle the bikini fitting himself, take photos of the samples on, and provide me with detailed notes for the factory. He was always at the fittings. If something fit wrong, he took the necessary measurements and followed up with production notes to the factory. Part of his job was to give the factory feedback on sample fit. He needed to make certain that the sample measurements matched the original size specs, which were given to the factory along with our swimwear CADs (computer-aided designs).

But Todd called in sick too.

So, late that afternoon, I dragged myself to the fitting, where the model tried on eight new bikini samples. I took measurements and photos, all while wishing I was curled up in bed with a cup of hot tea.

I was already annoyed I'd had to come in and work while I was sick, but what truly disturbed me was that Todd was too foolish to make his social media posts private. I could see with my own two eyes that he had gone to a destination wedding with his boyfriend and was enjoying a long weekend away instead of working and helping with the fitting. He did not look the least bit sick in those photos.

All our employees received a certain amount of personal time off—PTO days—to be used however they chose. Todd could have used one! But instead, he just lied.

Things slowly escalated from there....

CHAPTER 22

THE MONEY HEIST

O N ANOTHER OCCASION, I GAVE Todd the fabrics and designs he needed to drop off at our sample maker in the city for a couple special one-off runway designs. These were exclusive for the upcoming Swim Week fashion show. For some strange reason, Todd told the sample maker, incorrectly, that she didn't need to sew the straps onto either bikini top. He decided, independently, that he was going to make the bikini straps custom fit both runway models—which was absurd, considering the chaos that ensued at every show.

We *always* have to switch a few models, even when we request to book specific ones for each of our runway shows. At the end of the day, you don't know if you're going to get the exact models you choose at casting. Sometimes there are scheduling conflicts with other fashion shows or bookings. That's just how it works—and he knew that.

On the other hand, Todd knew how to sew, and he assured me he'd sew the straps on both bikini tops by the time we needed them, so I swallowed my growing exasperation.

I took the team out for dinner as usual. But Todd kept ordering drinks and driving up the tab. I was appalled he was ordering off the more expensive cocktail menu, as if he was entitled. As the night wrapped up, Todd announced he was going on a walk because he needed fresh air.

"Don't you still need to sew?" I asked, with more than a hint of malice.

"I'll do that later, don't you worry," he said.

The next day, I headed over to the salon to get my hair blown out. It's probably the one time a year I get my hair done—because it's Miami and because it's like a steam bath outside in July.

As I settled in for a moment of pampering, Todd walked through the door.

He came over to talk to me. And I noticed he was sewing as he took a seat next to me.

"Oh my God, what are you doing? You should be done with those bikini tops by now!"

"I'll get it done, don't worry, Jen," he said.

But when we met again that afternoon, only a few hours before the runway show was supposed to start, he was still sewing. Now he was freaking out too. The intern who came down to Miami with us tried to help Todd, but he screamed that he could do it himself.

The fashion show was starting in an hour. As always, we had to replace a few of the models, including one who was wearing a one-off bikini. It was total chaos, and it needn't have been.

In the end, I don't know how many people noticed, but one model sported a bikini bottom with one side laced up with the bow tied on the top and the other side laced down with the bow tied on the bottom. I will never forget how angry I felt when I saw the professional fashion show images afterwards and realized it.

Despite all this, at the afterparty and while completely drunk, Todd had the nerve to tell some random people that *he* designed *my* entire bikini collection! He should have kept in mind that I saved all my original sketches, research, and design inspiration on my personal laptop.

That was an early warning sign I should have never ignored.

Shockingly, Todd later tried to steal information from our company. He was downloading files to an external hard drive from the desktop computer in his office—something his contract forbade him to do.

A maintenance employee at our office building was the first to inform us about Todd's sneaky ways. One morning, he pulled Russell and I aside to talk.

"You guys know Todd, right?" he asked.

Well, of course we did; the guy worked for us.

"Yeah, we know him," I said.

"Well, he comes here super early in the morning before you guys get in, then he goes back out to get coffee or whatever and returns after you arrive," he said. "It seems like he's up to something no good."

Then it clicked.

Todd might have been trying to steal proprietary information from the company. His boyfriend—the bad influence—may also have helped to con us out of $100,000.

We'd recently had an issue with a wire transfer to our factory in China. Normally, we paid the factory a portion of what we owed at the beginning of production. We made another large payment halfway through the process, and then we'd pay the balance at the end when the goods were released from China and shipped off to the States.

Russell had been about to go wire the funds as he usually did after receiving an invoice, but he received an email from our factory saying that their bank account had changed and that he needed to wire the money to a new account. This seemed odd, and Russell questioned it. He emailed the factory manager to confirm the new bank account information. Honestly, he didn't think to text or call her instead.

Russell, bless his heart, has never been very skeptical or tech savvy. Of the two of us, he's also the one who's more likely to give everyone the benefit of the doubt. After receiving the email confirming the new bank account, Russell headed to the bank and wired the $100,000 payment we owed. To our bewilderment, the factory continued to send emails saying they were still expecting payment.

That's when it all came crashing down. The money had actually been wired to an account in London. Of course, by the time we figured this out with Wells Fargo, the money was gone, and the fraudulent bank account had been closed. One of the dads of the boys who played lacrosse with Josh worked for the FBI. He referred us to a colleague of his, who worked in the FBI Cyber Division, to give us advice. The agent normally worked on huge corporate cases, so this was small change for him, but he agreed to help us however he could. After reviewing all the emails traded back and forth prior to the wire transfer and the back end of the email logs, he told us it appeared the factory's email had been hacked. He suggested it was most likely a tactic called a Man-in-the-Middle Attack (MITM). This type of attack occurs anytime a hacker transmits emails between two people who think they are communicating directly. When emails are traded between two people, unless they both use encryption, the communication is left open and can be intercepted and read by anyone.[24]

Someone else had been emailing us, pretending to be answering from the factory.

The agent said the email was most likely hacked by someone outside the factory, but he couldn't tell us for certain that it was not an inside job. This was beyond crazy! How would we ever get our money back? Even though we told the factory what the FBI agent explained about the email being hacked and about the bank account in London, the factory still demanded to be paid.

With a bit of internet sleuthing on social media, I discovered Todd's boyfriend had been in London, shopping at a bunch of high-end boutiques I knew that he couldn't afford—he worked for minimum wage at a retail store in the Village, downtown New York.

That certainly didn't prove anything, but it sure looked suspect considering the circumstances.

We moved quickly so Todd didn't have time to do any damage control. I called and asked our IT expert to come and check Todd's computer. We told all the employees he was coming to do some updates, and then he went straight for Todd's desktop first. Todd had no time to cover his tracks before the IT guy backed everything up on our office Time Machine—an external storage device for all of the company's Macs—and then found the portable hard drive still connected to his desktop with a USB cable.

We called Todd into my office. He tried to deny that he was stealing information, made excuses, and claimed he was innocent. But even if Todd *hadn't* been part of the money disappearing (that was conjecture), he was still downloading our company information illegally and breeching his employment contract. We terminated him on the spot.

The very next day, our e-commerce website was hacked with extremely graphic webcam porn. I was horrified—anyone shopping online for our swimwear could see it. Children could see it! Our lawyer sent Todd a cease and desist letter, but it took hours for our graphic designer to get the smut taken down.

This whole thing really pissed me off. Todd was someone I once trusted. He'd been to my house, I'd taken him out for dinner, and we'd even been for drinks now and then when we had meetings in the city. We were good to him. Even though I'd been betrayed by others in the business, this felt intensely personal.

Looking back, I don't know that I could have foreseen any of it without some serious help from a crystal ball. Todd was such a different person when he first started working for us. He had a different work ethic. Sometimes people get into situations or relationships that bring out the very worst versions of themselves.

To this day, I believe that's what happened with Todd. But what was I going to do? Tell every new single employee that they couldn't date or fraternize with anyone? Of course not. At the end of the day, this experience didn't deter us from looking for the best in our employees and giving them a chance—but it did teach me the value in dropping deadweight fast.

CHAPTER 23

SEAL OF APPROVAL

AT THE NEXT SURF EXPO, I found another factory for us to work with. It seemed like we needed a fresh start after the last debacle. They had some sample boardshorts on display, so I asked to see them. They'd clearly worked with large boardshort companies before, apparent from the logos on the samples, and their swimwear was well made. Carefully examining the boardshorts, I could recognize quality fabric and workmanship.

There's a difference between engineered prints and random prints. Random prints, such as stars, watermelons, sharks, etc., are easier to execute on apparel like boardshorts. But engineered prints are more difficult because of the controlled position of artwork. A good deal of planning and exact measurements is required for engineering a print. The fabric is cut differently, and there is more waste. You recognize a quality garment when the stripes align across a seam. Engineered prints are harder, and the process is more labor intensive. A good factory should be able to execute engineered prints well.

After the trade show was over, I asked this factory to make us some samples to find out if they could deliver quality product with our specs. And deliver they did. Their samples were far superior to anything we'd seen with the previous factory.

It's hard to switch factories, especially when you apply specialized technology in your garment. It feels like changing caretakers for your kids. There's a tremendous amount of detail you have to review for product development with a new factory and so much you have to instruct them on about your tech packs, your time and action calendar (T&A), your packaging requirements, and shipping. You have to calculate pricing, whether it's LDP— "landed duty paid" or FOB—"free on board," where the buyer is responsible for all import and shipping fees. From the specific production itself to how you want the end product packaged, it can be extremely time consuming and a big undertaking to make the switch. Prior to new production, there is a series of development samples. Proto samples, fit samples, and size set samples must be made and approved before anything else can move forward with a new factory. Even then, there are still numerous sets of garment samples that must be approved by the customer prior to mass production. It took much longer than a few weeks for a new factory to get up and running with our product line.

But, ultimately, making the transition paid off. They got it right, and I no longer had to waste time painstakingly going over Pantone colors or correcting numerous sample measurements.

For weeks, I heard nothing about the patent. But, finally, the silence ended with an email notification.

I opened the email immediately. I needed to know, even if the truth hurt. My breath hitched in my chest when I saw the words: *Notice of Allowance: approved.*

A rush of joy flooded through me. I had fought so hard to get to this point—from figuring out how to fix the problem of not being able to find boardshorts with adjustable waistbands to designing a quality product to proving to people I could run my own successful business. I'd received the official stamp of approval. We filed for the first patent in April 2011 and were finally awarded it in May 2013.

It hadn't been that long ago when my dad had said, "You'll never get a patent." He didn't think the idea could ever take off. I'd never been so happy to prove him wrong.

I picked up the phone and called him.

"I got the patent," I said. "Isn't that great?"

"Well, do you want a plaque for your office?" he said, somewhat sarcastically.

"Yes. I believe I do," I replied. And that was the end of that.

He never said he was proud, even after my victory.

Russell and I took our entire staff out to celebrate at Roots Steakhouse, a fancy New York-style chophouse that boasts a long mahogany bar framed with brass rails. Tables were covered with white tablecloths. Waiters in black uniforms and white aprons served guests with French-style cart service.

So much of our journey had been an uphill battle, but things were finally looking up.

My mom told me a couple times that my dad was proud of me. Maybe he said it to her, but he never said it to me. He passed away in December 2017, so I can only take her word for it.

Still, the more he and others doubted me, the more it made me determined. I've always had the kind of personality that thrives under pressure. I know a lot of people would have just given up. But I grew up in a tough household, and that prepared me for the future. As I got older, I decided that I wasn't going to let anyone make me feel bad and bring me down.

At this point, I've been on national television. I've had magazine articles written about me. I've had my own fashion shows and attended exclusive parties. But this journey was never about that. I would compare it to someone who wanted to climb Mount Everest. You hear about these mountaineers, and you might think they're crazy. Yet, they train and put themselves through grueling hardship in order to succeed. It's one of the hardest things in the world to do. I consider it to be similar to running your own business. It's unquestionably hard to launch a business and keep it going. Not only that, but you also feel as if you truly accomplished something because you went up against challenges and adversity. Climbers go up against the ice and snow equipped with oxygen and their own determination. I got two patents and won a frivolous fight about a trademark because I was equally determined to do what I set out to do.

My joy stemmed purely from how it felt to achieve my goal. The rest was icing on the cake. I was happy that my husband and kids felt proud of me. I was proud that my boardshorts were on the racks and shelves of retail stores and that people could go out and buy them.

I launched our bikini line in 2016. I wanted to design a collection of separates that combined performance with a sexy, feminine flair.

By this point, Just Bones Boardwear was in luxury resorts and fine hotels. We were in the Ritz Carlton, the Hilton, the Loews, the Four Seasons, and additional hotels across the States, including the U.S. Virgin Islands. We were also in a few international hotels.

I'd spoken to the buyers at the Atlantis, who'd shown interest in our boardshorts previously, but they'd told me that everything had to be customized for the resort. Therefore, because so much of production with the first factory had been outside of my control and went through our agent, we couldn't swing it. We couldn't meet their specific needs. Our agent never made life any easier. But when we switched factories, everything changed.

It took me three years to land the Atlantis account, but I did it—despite so many initial setbacks.

It always felt exciting for people to recognize our brand, but this was different. With *this* account, it felt like things had come full circle. Years after I'd scoured the shops around the Atlantis looking for swimwear that would work for my family, my own boardshorts were going to be on sale at the resort. Later on, Atlantis employees told us that we always met their criteria flawlessly with the resort's ticketing, packaging, and shipping guidelines and that we made their jobs easy and were consistently pleasant to deal with. That felt good to hear after years of trying to win them over.

If I could go back in time and give myself some advice, I'd tell myself not to be so nervous when we first launched. I'd tell myself to listen to my own instincts and make changes when I thought they were valuable ones.

I'd listened to other people who gave poor advice for too long. I knew we should have changed factories earlier. That agent dragged us down and held us back. Had we made the switch sooner, I'm convinced we could have grown faster. Other factories had always been available, but as new business owners in a new industry, we didn't know what we didn't know. At the time, with so many other things going on between the auto accident and the trademark lawsuit, we simply couldn't see what other options we had.

Over time, and in lieu of having a crystal ball, I learned to trust myself and my intuition.

CHAPTER 24

THE CROSSING

I N 2016, MILLBURN FINALLY DECIDED to act in the interest of pedestrians and went through with serious changes to the traffic patterns as part of the Complete Streets program. To accomplish the heavy lifting of lane changes, sidewalk bump-outs and more, the township had to commit more than $8 million to the initiative.[25]

However, the program faced opposition from those who couldn't see the immediate benefits. Between business owners protesting and politicians losing their seats for supporting the plan, it got ugly.

There were people angry about changes to the parking situation and the inconvenience such a large project inevitably causes. And, of course, I had to listen to people complain about it.

Someone even came up to me and said, "They did this because of you, you know."

I didn't know how to reply. How about all the other accidents that had happened in the town? How about the fact that these changes would make the town safer and maybe even save a life?

For the longest time, I couldn't think about walking near that intersection. But, in late 2018—*six years* after my accident—I finally found the courage to walk through town and stand on the corner where my life had changed.

My therapist had been trying to convince me to face that intersection for a long time, but I'd resisted. She said it was a big part of my healing process and treating my PTSD. I felt like it was a death sentence. I thought it was brave enough for me to keep working in that town, even though I took a shortcut while driving to my office to avoid that intersection. Truth be told, my office was blocks away from that intersection.

I started to "face my demons" in little spurts. One day I was finally able to go to the Starbucks on the other corner and get a coffee. I could see the intersection right through the window. My heart pounded wildly.

For a while, that was enough. Then I convinced myself to get closer to the intersection. I wouldn't cross it, but I got close, skirting around the corner, my body clinging to the buildings along the sidewalk.

Weeks passed until I was able to take a bigger step.

I still couldn't bring myself to cross at that actual intersection, but I did navigate my way across at a parallel one.

My heart was racing the entire time, but I put one. Foot. In. Front. Of. The. Other and found myself moving forward. I faced my fear and my trauma, and I crossed the street. Sure, my heart was a jackhammer, and my palms were waterfalls, but I felt brave. I felt strong.

Most of all, I knew I hadn't given up or given in to fear.

CHAPTER 25

CASTLES IN THE AIR

I T'S STRANGE NOW, LOOKING BACK. I can't help but wonder sometimes what I could have done had the accident never happened. Would my business be on a completely different trajectory?

But I know now that there are things in life that happen outside our control, and we must simply do our best to adapt. Maybe these things even prepare us for what else may come our way.

When I was pregnant, I had to be on bed rest for three months due to preterm labor. Back then, there was no Uber Eats or DoorDash. There was no Netflix or Amazon Prime Video. Russell and my friends all still worked. I was bored out of my mind watching Lifetime movies. With the accident, I had to change the way I worked.

I underwent unpleasant surgeries.

I've been stuck in so many situations that I had zero choice about being in.

Back then, I coped by diving into the work I loved. In a way, I think my company saved me. If I hadn't had something to do back then, something to give me purpose even though I was struggling, I don't know where I'd be now.

If I buried myself in work, in deadlines, and in emails, I didn't have to face all the other things going on in my life. It was a coping strategy for me.

The more work I did, the less I had time to think about everything else that was bothering me. Sometimes I wonder if that was an unhealthy approach—but was it really all that bad? Without the job I loved, I might have stayed in bed doing nothing.

Those major life events built up my tolerance for relinquishing control.

In 2020, many people experienced that kind of helplessness for the first time with the coronavirus pandemic.

I decided not to do an in-person trade show in January 2021. I've made many sacrifices with my own health for my business, but this was different. I couldn't live with the idea of asking someone else to risk their safety and well-being for the sake of my business.

So, I learned to cope differently. When the world shut down, I still got up every morning, got dressed, did my hair, and put my makeup on. I made the bed, with all the decorative throw pillows, every day.

When I find myself frustrated with loved ones around me now struggling with depression and anxiety, I realize their coping mechanisms are just different than mine.

I may not fully understand what they're going through. I might want to scream, "Get your act together. Get out of bed to do something, and you'll feel better!"

But I know better than to judge others for how they choose to cope—especially after experiencing a life-changing event.

———————

At this point, there have been companies that copied my idea, though they changed their design enough not to violate my patents. Until I created Just Bones Boardwear, there was nothing like it on the market. But three or four years later, a few of the big brands in swimwear got on the bandwagon.

When I first started seeing similar products available, I was furious. I'd worked so hard to win my patents and resolve that trademark lawsuit, and I was still fighting to put the car accident behind me. There was so much going on, and running a business was not for the faint of heart. I wanted my lawyer to do something about it. I wanted to be able to stop these corporate giants from benefiting from my idea.

One major surf company even took my trademarked slogan, "Reinventing the Boardshort," and slapped it across the landing page for their online store. They agreed to phase it out after my lawyer contacted theirs.

I kept thinking, *you have this huge marketing department, yet you can't come up with your own branding ideas?*

I had finally penetrated the market and had a decent customer base, and now these guys thought they could swoop in and steal my ideas just because they were bigger. Back then, it made my blood boil!

Now, however, I can view it as a form of flattery—you know what they say about imitation.

Adjustable waist boardshorts will continue to improve people's everyday enjoyment of water sports and many outdoor activities. They fit better so you feel more comfortable. And you don't need to worry about wardrobe malfunctions!

Beyond providing the perfect fit for growing young boys and men in-between sizes, Just Bones Boardwear helps surfers, wakeboarders, and kiteboarders keep their boardshorts secure and from falling down in challenging conditions—like big wave surfing or while competing.

Perhaps the most impactful aspect is the difference they can make for families who have children with special needs. Moms with special needs children have told us that our adjustable waist boardshorts make family trips to the beach more manageable and more fun. It has freed them to enjoy the experience in ways they couldn't before.

Nothing makes me happier than making another mom's life easier—that was my mission after all. It simply puts a smile on my face.

CHAPTER 26

REINVENTING MYSELF AGAIN

IMAGINED I'D FINISH MY CAREER in the fashion industry by licensing my patents. Then I could spend my days golfing, hiking, doing yoga, and hanging out by the pool. Maybe I'd be available for consulting if anyone needed my expertise. As it happens, one company offered that scenario to me a couple years ago—I could have been done working full-time and just collected royalty checks from then onward.

And then the coronavirus pandemic hit, leaving large segments of the apparel industry—especially brick-and-mortar retail stores—reeling.

In 2020, several big-name retail brands such as J.C. Penney, J. Crew, Neiman Marcus, Brooks Brothers, Lord & Taylor, Tailored Brands, and Century 21 filed for bankruptcy.[26] While some of those brands may make it through to the other side after reorganizing, many won't. Some experts even projected between 20%–30% of retail brands would either close for good or sell.[27] The retail landscape was already changing prior to the pandemic with people moving more and more to online shopping, but this trend has been immensely accelerated.

Experts estimate that customers will continue to rely on shopping online long after the pandemic. Although people were already taking fewer trips to the mall, brick-and-mortar stores will have to revolutionize their business practices if they want people to keep coming in. That might mean, according to the *Harvard Business Review*, that retailers will benefit more from hosting events rather than simply holding merchandise. Equally, if retailers don't create a smooth e-commerce experience, they could be in trouble as well.[28]

I don't know what the post-apocalyptic world will look like. At the very least, I don't think companies will rely on in-person trade shows like we used to. I don't believe these events will ever be quite the same post-pandemic, as there are so many travel and political issues involved.

Recently, I met with a friend and mentor who's been in the game for a long time. He's in his 70s and much more of a business expert than I'll ever be. He's been on the board of multiple companies, and he really knows how to speak to people. He told me that the key to being successful in any business, especially in the long term, is being able to pivot in times of crisis. To survive, you have to be willing to change with the times.

Where does that leave us?

It's hard to say for sure. Just Bones Boardwear will have to pivot again, as many companies have, to keep up with the continuously changing retail landscape. I don't yet know what that means—but that's okay.

Just Bones Boardwear has historically functioned as a wholesaler, selling direct to retail businesses. The fact of the matter is, at the time of writing this book, I have buyers who are losing their jobs permanently or are on furlough indefinitely. They don't know if or when they're going back to work due to closures, some which were mandated. Obviously, that puts a kink in the supply chain.

We're in the process of figuring out how to best revamp our online store and pivot to selling more direct to consumer. It's a big change, but I see that being the future of our business success.

Our company was founded with adjustment in mind. The current business climate represents the need for a new adjustment.

I've seen firsthand how well it can work when you're able to be flexible during a crisis. A girlfriend of mine was furloughed from a major apparel company at the beginning of the pandemic. The company lost millions of dollars as buyer after buyer canceled orders amid news of a global shutdown. She didn't know what she was going to do, but then she discovered a need. She was well connected with factories in China, so early on she pivoted to selling PPE (personal protective equipment) here in the U.S.—even to some government institutions. That has worked out undeniably well for her!

I've made a point to focus on personal growth also. I joined a community of entrepreneurs, from all types of industries, who are dedicated to helping each other, sharing ideas, and talking about triumphs and challenges they experience in business. Every so often, we make short introductions, describe our business, and more importantly, explain what we have to offer. The group hosts numerous interesting and prestigious speakers, who have founded or controlled some of the most successful companies in the U.S. It's always stimulating since each speaker provides a fresh perspective on business practices and what worked for them.

To stay the course, even in uncertain times, I think we can all start with two basic strategies: 1) Be willing to ask for help and advice. It doesn't make you stupid, weak, or unworthy—it makes you smart; 2) Be willing to offer help and share your knowledge with others.

I'm not saying I'm perfect. All you can do is keep trying to climb that mountain. Don't give up.

This past year has been far from normal. I don't have any solid answers about where we're going—the sand is shifting beneath our feet like the ocean tides. But I've faced big obstacles before. I've never been afraid to fail if I went down fighting. That was true when I was a teenager trying to get into FIT, it was true when I first launched this business, and it's true now. No matter what happens, I can rest easy knowing that I gave this thing my all.

I've learned it's okay to admit you don't know how your story will end—none of us really do. At the end of the day, I'll know I recognized a problem and threw everything I had into solving it. Ultimately, that's all I set out to do. I never set out to build a fashion empire.

Years ago, one of the stay-at-home moms tried to insult me. *You're always reinventing yourself, aren't you?*

At the time, I was annoyed with the backhanded compliment. But looking back, she's right. I *am* always reinventing myself. I've come to see it as a good thing. If I hadn't been able to grow and change, I'm not sure I could have overcome and survived the lawsuit, the car accident, or the fashion industry. I now see it as my greatest strength.

ACKNOWLEDGMENTS

I AM FOREVER GRATEFUL TO MY father, who put the fire in my belly to go after my boardshort patents. He is greatly missed. I'm eternally indebted to the doctor, (whomever you are) who raced to save my life immediately after my accident. I hope you will read this one day.

I also sincerely thank all of the doctors and medical professionals who contributed to my lengthy recovery and rehabilitation. I owe you a debt of gratitude.

My dear friends, Winnie, Lori, Stacy, Jenny, Joy, Janet, Linda, Minerva, Dorrie, Doug and Nick—your help and support never wavered while I launched and grew my business, and I will always be thankful.

Many thanks to my legal team for their faith in me, their sheer perseverance and commitment to always getting the job done. Without you, we would be "Just Boardwear," and I could not endlessly annoy my family by telling them I'm an inventor.

I would be remiss in not recognizing the part these amazing people played in the success of my brand; they saw something and gave me a chance. Thank you Judy, Kathy, Jane, Celia, Trish, Molly, Colleen, Chandra, and Susan. And thanks a million to these fabulous humans for their endless support—Mom, Rebecca, Monica, Paul, Sandra, Don, Suzanne, Randi, Chris, Rod, and Tracy.

I would not even be writing this page without the infinite hours of dedication and work of this incredible team who helped me bring this memoir to fruition. I offer my endless gratitude to Tim, Kelly, Jaqueline and Julie.

Lastly, I must express my utmost appreciation and recognition to Jeanine and Diane. You helped me stay strong when I felt weak, you helped me realize my greatest potential, and you helped me believe.

JBW

ENDNOTES

1 Dana Feldman, "Shark Week 2019 Delves Deep into the Importance Of Conserving Shark Species Worldwide," *Forbes*, July 25, 2019, https://www.forbes.com/sites/danafeldman/2019/07/25/shark-week-2019-delves-deep-into-the-importance-of-conserving-shark-species-worldwide/?sh=28f41fa524a5.

2 "Post-Traumatic Stress Disorder (PTSD)," Mayo Clinic, July 6, 2018, https://www.mayoclinic.org/diseases-conditions/post-traumatic-stress-disorder/symptoms-causes/syc-20355967.

3 Ibid.

4 Ibid.

5 "Student Struck by Vehicle as She Crosses Road to Colonial Cemetery," *The Item of Millburn and Short Hills*, May 17, 2012, A2, https://www.newspapers.com/image/499682252.

6 Ibid.

7 Ibid.

8 "Time to Act on Downtown 'Racecourse,'" *The Item of Millburn and Short Hills*, July 12, 2012, A4, https://www.newspapers.com/image/499683423.

9 Ibid.

10 Lindsey Kelleher, "Stop & Shop Pressed on Design and Safety," *The Item of Millburn and Short Hills*, August 9, 2012, A1–2, https://www.newspapers.com/image/499683952.

11 "Police: Accidents in Town and Around," *The Item of Millburn and Short Hills*, September 20, 2012, A3, https://www.newspapers.com/image/499684555.

12 Harry Trumbore, "Police Not Wild about 3-Way Stop at Glen and Lackawanna," *The Item of Millburn and Short Hills*, February 23, 2012, A1 and A3, https://www.newspapers.com/image/499680612.

13 Diane Oriente, "Stop the Speeding in the Center of Town," *The Item of Millburn and Short Hills*, June 12, 2013, A4, https://www.newspapers.com/image/499618402.

14 Cecilia Levine, "Pedestrian Safety Problems Persistt," *The Item of Millburn and Short Hills*, March 19, 2015, A1–2, https://www.newspapers.com/image/499625794.

15 Ibid.

16 "Complete Streets History," Township of Millburn New Jersey, accessed May 26, 2021, https://www.twp.millburn.nj.us/327/Project-History.

17 Ibid.

18 "Dangerous by Design 2021," Smart Growth America, accessed May 26, 2021, https://smartgrowthamerica.org/dangerous-by-design/.

19 Ibid.

20 Ibid.

21 Danielle DeSisto, "Experts Answer Complete Streets Q's," *The Item of Millburn and Short Hills*, February 18, 2016, A1–2, https://www.newspapers.com/image/499676549.

22 Ibid.

23 Danielle DeSisto, "Project Causes Headaches," *The Item of Millburn and Short Hills*, August 25, 2016, A1–2, https://www.newspapers.com/image/499679887.

24 Rick Kuwahara, "Top 3 Ways Email Gets Hacked," Paubox, November 15, 2015, https://www.paubox.com/blog/top-3-ways-email-gets-hacked/.

25 "Let's Think Complete Streets," *The Item of Millburn and Short Hills*, March 31, 2016, https://www.newspapers.com/image/499677545.

26 Scott Reeves, "COVID-19 Pandemic Has the Fashion Industry Reeling," *Newsweek*, November 2, 2020, https://www.newsweek.com/covid-19-pandemic-has-fashion-industry-reeling-1544103.

27 Ibid.

28 Denise Lee Yohn, "The Pandemic Is Rewriting the Rules of Retail," *Harvard Business Review*, July 6, 2020, https://hbr.org/2020/07/the-pandemic-is-rewriting-the-rules-of-retail.